Briefly: Plato's
The Republic

David Mills Daniel

scm press

© David Mills Daniel 2006

The Author has asserted his right under the Copyright, Designs and
Patents Act, 1988, to be identified as the Author of this Work

The author and publisher acknowledge material reproduced from
Plato, *The Republic*, translated by H. D. P. Lee, second edition (revised),
re-issued with new Further Reading, London: Penguin Books, 2003,
ISBN 0140449140. Reproduced by permission of Penguin Books Ltd.
All rights reserved.

British Library Cataloguing in Publication data

A catalogue record for this book is available
from the British Library

0 334 04034 5/978 0 334 04034 7

First published in 2006 by SCM Press
9–17 St Alban's Place,
London N1 0NX

www.scm-canterburypress.co.uk

SCM Press is a division of
SCM-Canterbury Press Ltd

Printed and bound in Great Britain by
Bookmarque Ltd, Croydon, Surrey

Contents

Contents

iv

Introduction

The SCM *Briefly* series is designed to enable students and general readers to acquire knowledge and understanding of key texts in philosophy, philosophy of religion, theology and ethics. While the series will be especially helpful to those following university and A-level courses in philosophy, ethics and religious studies, it will in fact be of interest to anyone looking for a short guide to the ideas of a particular philosopher or theologian.

Each book in the series takes a piece of work by one philosopher and provides a summary of the original text, which adheres closely to it, and contains direct quotations from it, thus enabling the reader to follow each development in the philosopher's argument(s). Throughout the summary, there are page references to the original philosophical writing, so that the reader has ready access to the primary text. In the Introduction to each book, you will find details of the edition of the philosophical work referred to.

In *Briefly: Plato's The Republic*, we refer to Plato, *The Republic*, translated by Desmond Lee, second edition (revised), reissued with new Further Reading, London: Penguin Books, 2003, ISBN 0140449140.

Each *Briefly* begins with an Introduction, followed by a chapter on the Context in which the work was written. Who was this writer? Why was this book written? With Some Issues to Consider, and some Suggestions for Further Reading, this *Briefly* aims to get anyone started in their philosophical investigation. The detailed summary of the philosophical work is followed by a concise chapter-by-chapter Overview and an extensive Glossary of terms.

Bold type is used in the Detailed Summary and Overview sections to indicate the first occurrence of words and phrases that appear in the Glossary. The Glossary also contains terms used elsewhere in this *Briefly* guide and other terms that readers may encounter in their study of Plato's *The Republic*.

Traditionally, Plato's *The Republic* is divided into ten Books. However, H. D. P. Lee's translation of *The Republic*, on which this Briefly is based, divides it into eleven Parts. Readers who want more information about the traditional division of *The Republic* should refer to Lee's translation.

Context

Who was Plato?

Plato was born, around 429 BC, into a leading Athenian family. His parents were Ariston and Perictione, and he had two elder brothers, Adeimantus and Glaucon, who feature in the *The Republic*. This was an important period in Athens' history. Under Pericles' leadership, it had developed its democratic institutions, while its formidable navy, which had played a crucial part in defeating the Persian invasions of Greece, had enabled it to build up a large empire. But Athenian success caused tensions with other Greek states, notably Sparta, Greece's leading military power; and, in 431 BC, the Peloponnesian War began. The failure of an Athenian expedition against Syracuse, in Sicily (415–412 BC), discredited the democratic politicians (lesser men than Pericles, who kept power by their influence over the Athenian Assembly), and led to political instability and violence. After Athens' defeat in 404 BC, Sparta supported a successful oligarchic revolution, but this brutal regime was short-lived and democracy was restored.

By this time, Plato had become a pupil of the philosopher, Socrates, who had devoted his life to the pursuit of truth, particularly in ethics. However, some Athenians found his challenges to conventional ideas offensive, and he was accused of undermining belief in the gods and corrupting youth. Plato was appalled when, on top of all the other terrible events he had witnessed, Socrates was tried and executed in 399 BC. Plato had been considering a political career, but now became disenchanted with politics and all existing forms of government. During the decade after Socrates' death, he travelled, served in the Athenian army and began to write. He developed the view, strongly expressed in *The Republic*, that states must be ruled by philosophers who, after rigorous intellectual training, will understand the true nature of goodness and justice, and thus govern well and in their subjects' interests; at the very least, existing rulers needed to become philosophers. He founded the Academy, the world's first university, in Athens, around 386 BC. It was designed as a place to train future philosopher rulers, and was attended by Aristotle. Plato devoted the rest of his life to teaching, and to writing books, in which he first recorded, and then developed, Socrates' thought (Socrates wrote nothing himself) and his own ideas. He died in 347 BC. Plato's contribution to the development of western philosophy is immense, and it is probably fair to say that he determined the issues it would address.

What is *The Republic*?

The Republic was probably written about 375 BC and, like his earlier books, is a dialogue, in which Socrates discusses philosophical ideas with one or more people. But, in these later books Plato, through Socrates, gives detailed exposition of his own views and/or interpretation and development of Socrates' teaching. Socrates' method of interrogating his interlocutors about their views, exposing flaws in their arguments, and thus clearing the philosophical ground, is confined to the early part of the book. *The Republic* is remarkable for the range of the philosophical issues it covers. These include: the nature of reality; the difference between knowledge and opinion;

the nature of justice; how we can know what is good and right; who should rule a state and how it should be governed; and the aim and content of education. It is also beautifully written.

The dialogue begins casually from a chance meeting between Plato and Polemarchus, a resident of the Piraeus, during a religious festival. Invited to Polemarchus' house, Plato chats with his father, Cephalus, who suggests that doing right consists of being truthful and always returning borrowed items. This broadens into a general discussion of the nature of justice, and whether or not a just man is happier than an unjust one, in which Socrates shows up the shortcomings of Polemarchus' conventional view that it is helping friends and injuring enemies, and Thrasymachus' cynical one that justice is (or, rather, is a name for) whatever is in the interests of the strongest: in particular, a government, the strongest power in a state. Thrasymachus makes his case belligerently, claiming that the strong, such as tyrants, whose behaviour (whatever it may be called) is actually unjust and who prey on others, are always better off and happier than their victims. Perhaps Socrates' most effective counter-argument is to show that even the worst people, like a gang of thieves, have to behave justly to each other, if they are to achieve a common objective.

At this point, the passages in which Socrates expounds Plato's ideas become longer (thus, it is convenient to refer to Socrates and Plato interchangeably), and Adeimantus and Glaucon become the only other interlocutors. They put forward a modified version of Thrasymachus' views. People want to prey on others, but are more afraid of being preyed upon, so justice is invoked to prevent either occurring. But people will always pursue their own interests, if they can get away with it. No one values justice in itself, and even its advocates do so on the grounds of the reputation and rewards (including heavenly ones) it brings. The hypocrisy goes further. The unjust are respected, provided they are sufficiently rich and powerful, and put on a show of respectability. They want Socrates to explain what justice is, and to show how practising it benefits the individual *per se*.

Socrates, professing not to know what justice is, suggests that it may be easier to identify in the state than the individual. He accepts Glaucon's objection that the primitive society with which he begins is not the same (and will not generate such complex ethical issues) as a civilized one, and indicates some of these: meeting demands for luxuries as well as necessities; the much wider range of different interests to be considered and satisfied; and the effects of territorial acquisitiveness. The implication seems to be that justice is easier to find, and follow, in a simple society. A civilized one will require both an army for defence and a whole governing and administrative class, whom Socrates refers to as 'Guardians'. Thus, Plato introduces one of *The Republic*'s key ideas: that an ideal state requires a professional ruling class, whose education and philosophical training equip its members to know what is good and right, and thus how to govern justly.

One of *The Republic*'s interesting characteristics is that, although it becomes increasingly didactic, the reader's sense of listening in on a real conversation is sustained by the way Socrates breaks off to explore ideas as they arise. At this point (Part III), he starts to discuss the Guardians' education, which must be balanced, involving both academic study and physical training, to develop self-discipline, character and initiative, as well as intellectual abilities. One thing Plato argues strongly for (and which has been fiercely criticized) is censorship. Books must serve the state's interests, by portraying the Greek gods and heroes as good and courageous, so students can model their own lives on their example. Greek drama and poetry, such as that of Homer, was widely used for educational purposes, and later in *The Republic* (Part X) Plato develops his criticisms of literature and its value, dismissing it as superficial, and condemning its encouragement of emotional self-indulgence. However, if literature's job is to serve the state, would this not apply to any intellectual pursuit, including philosophy? What would happen to Plato and his fellow philosophers in the ideal state he advocates?

Socrates explains (Part IV) that the Guardians divide into two groups, the oldest and most intelligent, who will be the Rulers, and the Auxiliaries, administrative assistants and professional soldiers. In contrast to the politicians (democrats and oligarchs) he had seen governing Athens, the Rulers' guiding principle must be always to do what is best for their community. Therefore, they must be free of temptations to pursue their own interests, and live communally and without private property. They must also prevent any extremes of wealth and poverty in the state, as these cause envy and rebellion. Plato makes it clear that the Guardians' happiness is not an important consideration: they exist to serve society, and to take care of its non-Guardian members. This society will be a just one because, with the consent of all members, it will be wisely governed by its Rulers, and bravely and effectively defended by its soldiers, leaving the rest of society (the businessman class) free to manage their businesses. He also suggests that this ideal society should develop a myth, to explain its origin and justify its structure. This has been condemned, both for advocating an official lie and for suggesting the permanently inferior position of a class(es) of society. But Plato does emphasize the Guardians' responsibility to review the abilities of the children in all three classes, and, if necessary, to move them to a different class.

Socrates concludes that this is what justice in society is: the members of its three classes sticking to their own jobs, and not taking on those for which others are better suited. He then argues that it is much the same thing in the individual who, like society, consists of three elements. If reason, assisted by spirit or the sense of indignation (aroused when desires impel a person to do what reason shows is wrong), controls the irrational appetite (where desires are located), the result will be a well-balanced, well-disciplined individual. Glaucon and Adeimantus agree that this shows that a life without justice and honour is not worth living.

Apart from the rather too convenient way in which Plato analyses the human personality into three elements, to match the three social classes, his account of what makes a well-disciplined and just individual is not likely to attract much dissent; but his views on society, whether considered in their historical context, or applied to the present, are more controversial. It would be generally accepted that modern society, with its complex political, economic and social problems and challenges, requires able and dedicated political leaders and professional administrators (a civil service), but it would not be thought possible or desirable to have a permanent ruling class, whose members have been educated for this role. And, while modern electorates want to see politicians putting society's interests above their own (and tend to feel they do not), it would be an intolerable restriction of individual freedom to require political leaders and administrators to live communally, and give up the right to own property, to make sure they do. But Plato's insistence that it is necessary for creating the ideal state must be judged in the light of his full account of the Guardians' way of life; what he thought was wrong with existing types of society; and the nature of reality and what rulers need to know to govern well.

In Part VI, Socrates turns aside from a proposed discussion of the shortcomings of existing societies, to respond to Adeimantus' request that he explain the full implications of the Guardians' communal way of living. What few would disagree with now (but few would have accepted then) is his view that, as there are no relevant intellectual or physical differences between men and women, the latter should have the same intellectual and physical training as men, and become Guardians (both Rulers and Auxiliaries). More controversial are his ideas about the Guardians' family life, or lack of it. They are not to have husbands and wives, but supervised by the Rulers, who must ensure that the most gifted Guardians breed most often, are to produce children for the state. These will be removed to state nurseries at birth, so that parents and children will not know each other, while any weak or defective children will be disposed of (this was practised in ancient Greece, particularly in Sparta). However, this whole section, which includes denial of family life to the Guardians, a strong emphasis on eugenics so that the Guardians breed what Plato calls a 'pedigree herd' (they will only be allowed to breed between their optimum ages for producing healthy children), provision for the disposal of unhealthy and unwanted children (Plato's references to this are evasive) and the arrangements for preventing incest among the Guardians, makes unpleasant reading.

Plato is explicit about the advantages. His ideal state's rulers and subjects will see each other as fellow citizens, as there will be none of the dissension caused when rulers make themselves rich, or promote their family interests (often at their subjects' expense), while unity among the Guardians will be guaranteed by their regarding themselves as members of one family. But who (then or now) would wish to belong to a ruling class at such a cost? The way of life Plato proposes for the Guardians goes against all the human instincts for permanent companionship and family life. And, even if the benefits were as clear-cut as he claims, and his system made rulers models of integrity, would a state be well governed by rulers who were as personally unhappy as Plato's Guardians are likely to be? One very understandable plea that Plato makes, arising from experience of the Peloponnesian War, is that the Greeks stop fighting and enslaving each other, and unite to defend themselves against barbarian threats, as they had during the Persian invasions.

So what was wrong with existing societies and forms of government? Plato groups them (Part IX) from the least bad (timarchy) to the worst (tyranny), and it is interesting that the former closely resembles the repressive and unattractive regime of Athens' enemy, Sparta, which was governed by a hereditary military oligarchy. For Plato, its great merit (in contrast to what he saw in Athens) is its respect for authority. However, two things (fatally) weaken it: the tendency to entrust government to soldiers, rather than the most intellectually able citizens, and the rulers' pursuit of individual wealth, which dissolves the unity of the ruling class, and leads to neglect of the needs of society; and this is the problem with any oligarchy. Of particular interest is what Plato says about democracy. He acknowledges its positive aspects, freedom and diversity, but warns of the dangers of excessive pursuit of individual liberty, which creates an undisciplined and lawless society, in which government is unable to enforce the law, and citizens refuse to obey it. As order breaks down, unscrupulous demagogues can take control, by convincing the people that they can sort out society's problems. At first, they just bribe the masses, but eventually impose a repressive tyranny. Plato has in mind direct democracy of the Athenian type, not modern representative democracy, but the process he describes is much like what occurred in inter-war Germany, and has happened elsewhere in recent history. It is unlikely that Plato would be satisfied with any democratic system, but what he has to say is a warning to democrats not to be complacent.

In Part VII, Plato makes absolutely explicit what Socrates has hinted at previously in *The Republic*: that the problems of existing states (and humanity) will not end until philosophers become kings, or current rulers become philosophers. Socrates concedes that this is a controversial view, and accepts the point that contemporary society may corrupt or distract philosophers, or so disgust them that they withdraw from it. However, he means the kind of philosophers who love their country; have characters that combine mental quickness and reliability; and who have reached the highest form of knowledge: the form of the good.

And this is why Plato maintains that only philosophers are fit to rule. He believes that that there are two orders of reality. Individual things in the ordinary, visible world, which are experienced through the senses, acquire their identity by being (in some way) copies of the unchanging forms of these things in an intelligible world, to which only the mind can give access. Thus, something is round by being a copy of, or participating in, the form of roundness. However, it will not be perfectly round, but will only approximate to roundness. Presiding over this intelligible world, and having the same relation to intelligible objects as the sun does to visible objects in the visible world, is the form of the good, the source of reality, truth and goodness. Those aware only of individual good things or just acts merely have opinions about what is good and just; knowledge is not attainable in the ordinary world of change and decay. Only those philosophers, who (after a long process of study and discussion: what Plato calls 'dialectic') have seen the essential nature of goodness, possess the highest form of knowledge; know what the good is in itself; and can say authoritatively which things and actions really are good, right and just. Thus, they must govern the state. This part of *The Republic* contains Plato's famous Simile of the Sun, which compares the form of the good to the sun; the Analogy of the Line, which provides further illustration of the two orders of reality and the states of mind that correspond to them; and the Simile of the Cave, which illustrates how the mind can ascend from the visible world to the intelligible one, and see the form of the good.

Not everyone accepts the view that there are two orders of reality, and that the ordinary world we experience through our senses is less real than an invisible, intelligible one. It runs counter to what common sense and sense experience tell us, and Plato does not explain how the intelligible and visible worlds relate to each other. However, for someone with this view of reality, philosophers will be the most important and useful people in the world, and the only ones qualified to govern.

In Part VIII, Plato describes the advanced studies, which will enable the trainee Guardians to see the form of the good. It involves concentrated study of mathematics, leading students to shift their focus away from the world of change; and dialectic, an intense programme of philosophical enquiry and discussion, which emphasizes use of the reason, and enables the mind to penetrate to the essential nature of things. Plato expects only the most able students to reach the final stage, and see the form of the good. They will become the Rulers, reluctantly taking turns to govern their state and train their successors, while devoting the rest of their time to their preferred occupation of philosophical study. Plato has admitted that making the Guardians happy is not a priority but, while the masses, ignorant of wisdom and truth, and ruled by their desires, pursue false pleasures, philosophers, who have penetrated to the intelligible world of unchanging and eternal truth, will lead lives guided by reason and knowledge.

Further, as the soul is immortal, the rewards of goodness and justice are not confined to this life; the just can look forward to all the blessings of heaven, while the unjust can expect the opposite. In Part XI, Plato develops his theory that the soul is pre-existent, as well as immortal, and so undergoes a cycle of rebirth, and reward and punishment.

It is possible to read *The Republic* and agree with almost none of it. We may consider that Plato's ideas about an intelligible world and the forms are fantastical and completely unsupported by experience; that we should decide what is right and wrong, or just and unjust, on the basis of how our actions meet human needs, or promote human happiness, not by reference to a form of the good that only a few will ever see; and that his theories about good government are a recipe for a totalitarian state, characterized by repression and censorship, and presided over by an irremovable ruling class. However, all who are interested in philosophy can learn from Plato's insistence, in *The Republic*, that the philosopher cannot accept that what appears to be true, or is generally accepted as being so, necessarily is. Whether in relation to the nature of reality, or questions of what is right or just, philosophical enquiry demands rigorous investigation and analysis of the issues before any conclusion is reached. Although we may think that the state Plato describes is far from ideal, it is hard to disagree with his view that the duty of those who take on the responsibility of governing or administering one, is to put the interests of the community they are serving above their own and to do what is best for its members. The range of philosophical issues *The Republic* covers is also remarkable, while it contains some striking passages, particularly, perhaps, the Similes of the Sun and the Cave.

Some Issues to Consider

- Polemarchus maintains that justice is helping friends and injuring enemies.
- Thrasymachus argues that justice is whatever is in the interests of the strongest, in particular a government, and that those who prey on others, such as tyrants, are always better off and happier than their victims.
- Socrates shows that even wicked people, like a gang of thieves, will be unable to achieve a common objective, unless they behave justly towards each other.
- Do people (always) pursue their own interests, if they can get away with it?
- Do we value justice in itself, or do we advocate behaving justly for the rewards and reputation doing so brings?
- In *The Republic*, Plato argues that the ideal state requires a professional ruling class, the Guardians, whose educational and philosophical training has equipped them to know what is good and right and how to rule justly.
- Plato wants books to serve the interests of the state by portraying Greek gods and heroes as good and courageous, so that students can follow their example in their own lives.
- There are two groups of Guardians: the Rulers, the oldest and most intelligent; and Auxiliaries, assistant administrators and professional soldiers.
- The Rulers must always do what is best for the community, and must not own private property, which might lead them to give priority to their own interests.
- Plato considers that justice in a society is the members of its three classes (Rulers, Auxiliaries and businessmen) sticking to their own jobs, and not attempting to do those for which others are better suited.
- Plato holds that, as there are no relevant intellectual or physi-

cal differences between men and women, women should have the same education as men and become Guardians.

- One of the Guardians' duties is to produce children who will serve the state as its future leaders.
- The Guardians will not be allowed to bring up, or even to know, their own children, in case they are tempted to use their positions to help their family.
- Would anybody want to be a Guardian?
- Would the way of living Plato proposes for the Guardians be a way of ensuring that political leaders and government administrators always served the state's interests, not their own?
- Plato wants the Greeks to stop fighting each other, and unite to defend themselves against barbarian threats.
- Is Plato right to say that there can be excessive pursuit of individual liberty in democracy, leading to an undisciplined and lawless society?
- Plato believes that the problems of existing states (and humanity) will not end until philosophers become kings, or current rulers become philosophers.
- Plato thinks there are two orders of reality: the ordinary, visible one that we experience through our senses, and the intelligible world, to which our minds give us access.
- The form of the good, the source of reality, truth and goodness, has the same relation to intelligible objects in the intelligible world, as the sun does to visible objects in the visible world.
- Only philosophers, who have seen the essential nature of goodness, know what the good is in itself and can say authoritatively what is good, right and just.
- Plato's programme of advanced studies for philosophers involves mathematics and dialectic, to enable the mind to penetrate to the essential nature of things.

- Are most people (unlike philosophers) ruled by their desires, leading them to pursue false pleasures?
- Plato holds that the soul is immortal, and that the just can look forward to all the blessings of heaven.

Suggestions for Further Reading

Plato, *The Republic*, trans. H. D. P. Lee, second edition (revised and reissued with new Further Reading), London: Penguin Books, 2003.

Plato, *The Republic of Plato*, trans. F. M. Cornford, Oxford and New York: Oxford University Press, 1945.

J. Annas, *An Introduction to Plato's Republic*, Oxford and New York: Oxford University Press, 1981.

K. J. Dover, *Greek Popular Morality in the Time of Plato and Aristotle*, Indianapolis: Hackett Publishing Company, 1994.

M. I. Finley, *The Ancient Greeks*, London: Penguin, 1991.

G. M. A. Grube, *Plato's Thought*, Indianapolis: Hackett Publishing Company, 1980.

N. Pappas, *Routledge Philosophy Guidebook to Plato and The Republic*, second edition, London and New York: Routledge, 2003.

N. P. White, *A Companion to Plato's Republic*, Indianapolis: Hackett Publishing Company, 1979.

N. P. White, *Plato on Knowledge and Reality*, Indianapolis: Hackett Publishing Company, 1976.

Detailed Summary of Plato's *The Republic*

Characters in the Dialogue (p. 2)
Socrates, Glaucon, Adeimantus, Polemarchus,
Cephalus, Thrasymachus of Chalcedon, Lysias,
Euthydemus, Niceratus, Charmantides and Cleitophon

Part I   Introduction (pp. 3–52)

1   *Prelude (pp. 3–8)*

Socrates: Yesterday, I went to **the Piraeus** with **Glaucon** for the festival of **Bendis**. We met **Polemarchus** and **Adeimantus** there, and Polemarchus invited us to his house. His father, **Cephalus**, was conducting a **sacrifice**, and I asked him whether old age is a 'difficult time of life' (p. 5).

Cephalus: Not for those who are 'sensible and good-tempered', but even youth 'is a burden' for those who are not (p. 5).

Socrates: Some would say that you 'carry your years lightly' because you are rich (p. 5).

Cephalus: There is some truth in that. It enables one to avoid 'unintentional cheating or lying' and leaving 'some debt to man unpaid' (p. 7).

Socrates: But does 'doing right' consist only in 'truthfulness and returning anything we have borrowed' (p. 7)?

Polemarchus: Yes, if we believe **Simonides**.

Cephalus: I must go back to my sacrifice. I shall leave you two to argue the matter out.

Detailed Summary of Plato's The Republic

2   The Conventional View of Justice Developed (pp. 8–15)

Socrates: What did Simonides say?

Polemarchus: That the right is giving 'every man his due' (p. 8).

Socrates: It cannot be that simple. For example, we would not give a friend back his weapon, if he had gone mad.

Polemarchus: Let us say, that what one friend owes to another is 'to do him good, not harm'; and what is due to enemies is 'an injury of some sort' (pp. 8–9).

Socrates: So what is the role of **justice**?

Polemarchus: To 'help and injure one's friends and enemies' (p. 9).

Socrates: But who are one's friends and enemies?

Polemarchus: Those one considers '**good**, honest men and the reverse' (p. 12).

Socrates: But we often make mistakes, thinking a man 'honest when he is not, and vice versa' (p. 12).

Polemarchus: Let us be more precise. A friend is 'one who both *seems* and *is* an honest man: while the man who seems, but is not, an honest man seems a friend, but really is not. And similarly for an enemy' (p. 12).

Socrates: So, 'it is just to do good to one's friend if he is good, and to harm one's enemy if he is **evil**' (p. 13). However, does a 'just man do harm to anyone' (p. 13)?

Polemarchus: Yes, to 'bad men' (p. 13).

Socrates: But if someone is harmed, does he not become 'worse by the standards of human excellence'; and is not 'justice human excellence' (p. 13)?

Polemarchus: Indeed.

Socrates: So harmed men will 'become more unjust', which would mean that just men were using their justice to 'make others unjust' (p. 13). Now, should 'good men use their goodness to make others bad' (p. 13)?

Polemarchus: That 'cannot be so' (p. 13).

Socrates: It is not 'the function of the just man to harm either his friends or anyone else', but that of the unjust one (p. 14). So, it is wrong to say justice is giving 'every man his due', if this means harming enemies and helping friends (p. 14). It is not right 'to harm anyone at any time' (p. 14).

3 Thrasymachus and the Rejection of Conventional Morality (pp. 15–40)

(a) First Statement and Criticisms (pp. 15–24)

Thrasymachus: Tell us 'what you think justice is' (p. 16). Give us 'a clear and precise definition' (p. 16).

Socrates: I am sorry, Thrasymachus, but 'I neither know nor profess to know anything about the subject' (p. 17).

Thrasymachus: So, this is the 'wisdom of Socrates: he won't teach anyone anything' (p. 18). Well, justice or right is 'simply what is in the interest of the stronger party' (p. 18). I am saying that '"right" is the same thing in all **states**, namely the interest of the established government', which is the 'strongest element in each state' (p. 19).

Socrates: You state that obeying those in power is right. However, if they get things wrong, the laws those in power pass may not be in their interests; but their subjects must still obey them, 'for that is what *right* is' (p. 19).

Thrasymachus: Of course.

Socrates: Which means that, if the rulers are mistaken, it will sometimes be right to do 'the opposite' of what is in the stronger party's interests (p. 19).

Cleitophon: Thrasymachus meant 'what the stronger *thinks* to be in his interest' (p. 20).

Socrates: Is that what you meant, Thrasymachus?

Thrasymachus: Certainly not. I would not call a mistaken

person '"stronger" just when he is making his mistake' (p. 21). As such, the ruler 'makes no mistake, and so infallibly enacts what is best for himself, which his subjects must perform' (p. 21). Thus, '"right" means the interest of the stronger party' (p. 21).

Socrates: Let us approach the question from a different angle. Thrasymachus, would you agree a **'professional skill'** does not look to any interest 'but its subject matter' (pp. 22–3)? For example, medicine is concerned with the interest of the body, not that of the doctor so, when the doctor prescribes it, his concern is not with 'his own interest but that of his patient' (p. 23).

Thrasymachus: Well, yes.

Socrates: So, does it not follow that 'no ruler of any kind, *qua* ruler, exercises his authority, whatever its sphere, with his own interest in view, but that of the subject of his skill': those he rules (p. 24)?

(b) Second Statement and Final Refutation (pp. 24–40)

Thrasymachus: Socrates, why does your nurse let you go 'drivelling round' in this way (p. 25)? Do shepherds look after their flocks for any other reason than 'the good of their masters and themselves' (p. 25)? Rulers feel the same way towards their subjects, and try to 'make a profit out of them' (p. 25). You must know that justice is someone else's good: that of the ruler 'at the expense of the subject' (p. 25). In any dealings between just and unjust, the latter always comes off better. And the ones who pursue their own advantage 'in a big way' prove how much better 'wrongdoing' and 'injustice' pay than doing right, and how their practitioners enjoy 'the highest happiness' (pp. 25–6). The **tyrant** engages in 'wholesale plunder', and is called 'happy and fortunate' by his subjects (p. 26). People only condemn wrongdoing because they fear 'suffering from it', not doing it (p. 26).

Socrates: I acknowledge that there are many unjust men committing crimes, but I am not convinced that 'injustice pays better than justice' (pp. 26–7). After all, you have shifted your ground. You accepted the definition of a 'true doctor', but now you say that a shepherd's priority is not the good of his flock (p. 27). However, his skill is 'devoted solely' to its welfare (p. 27). And I thought we had agreed it is the same with rulers. The doctor obviously does not expect to benefit personally from exercising his professional skill, as he expects payment for it. He does so because the benefit from exercising his professional skill goes to his patient, not himself. Therefore, we can say that every professional skill, including that of government, is exercised for the benefit of the subject, not the practitioner, and studies 'the interest of the weaker party and not the stronger' (p. 28).

Further, as good men will not want to be 'called mercenary', as a result of being paid for taking on government posts, 'in a **city** of good men there might well be as much competition to avoid power as there now is to get it, and it would be quite clear that the true ruler pursues his subjects' interest and not his own' (p. 29).

(i) The just man is wise and good, and the unjust man is bad and ignorant (pp. 30–4)

Socrates: But, Glaucon, what about Thrasymachus' claim that 'the unjust man has a superior life to the just' (p. 30)?
Glaucon: I think the just man's life 'pays the better' (p. 30).
Socrates: Well, Thrasymachus, would you agree that justice is 'an excellence' and 'injustice a fault' (p. 31)?
Thrasymachus: The opposite. Justice is 'supreme simplicity', especially if the unjust can take over the government of states, and give their wrongdoing 'full scope' (p. 31).
Socrates: The fact that you rank injustice with 'wisdom and

excellence', rather than saying that it is 'discreditable' but profitable, makes it harder to pursue our discussion, because we lack common ground (p. 31). However, would you agree that one just man will 'want to get the better of another' (p. 32)?

Thrasymachus: Indeed not. He would not then be the 'simple, agreeable man' I have described (p. 32).

Socrates: But he will with an unjust man. And will the unjust man compete with both the just and the unjust?

Thrasymachus: Of course. He wants 'more than his share in everything' (p. 32).

Socrates: So, the just man does not 'compete with his like, but only his unlike' (p. 32). However, the unjust man competes with 'both like and unlike' (p. 32). But the unjust man is the 'good sensible' one, and he is also '*like* others of his kind' (p. 32). Now, taking the 'whole range of professional knowledge', does anybody with such knowledge aim at 'anything more' than others with such knowledge (p. 33)?

Thrasymachus: I suppose not.

Socrates: However, the man who lacks knowledge will compete with both those who have knowledge, and those who do not. So, the man with professional knowledge is 'wise' and 'good', and will compete only with his opposite, not his like (p. 33). But the 'bad and ignorant man' will compete with both like and opposite (p. 33).

Thrasymachus: It seems so.

Socrates: But it was the unjust man who 'competes both with his like and his unlike', while the just man competed only with his unlike (p. 33). This means that the latter resembles the good man with knowledge, while the latter resembles 'the man who is ignorant and bad' (p. 34). Therefore, I conclude that 'the just man is wise and good, and the unjust bad and ignorant' (p. 34).

(ii) Injustice is a source of disunity and weakness (pp. 34–7)

Socrates: So, as 'justice implies excellence and knowledge', it should not be hard to show that it is 'stronger than injustice', which involves ignorance (p. 35). But let us consider a specific situation. Would an unjust state try to conquer another, and keep its people 'in subjection' (p. 35)?

Thrasymachus: Yes, and the most efficient and unjust state would be 'the most likely to do so' (p. 35).

Socrates: But will not the aggressor state require justice in order to succeed?

Thrasymachus: Only if, as you claim, 'justice involves knowledge' (p. 35)?

Socrates: But surely, no 'group of men', be they an army or 'thieves', can succeed in wrongdoing, 'if they wrong each other' (p. 35)? Doing so causes 'hatred and dissension' (p. 35).

Thrasymachus: I suppose so.

Socrates: So, as injustice produces 'factions and quarrels', it makes co-operative effort impossible, while leaving the individual 'incapable of action because of internal conflicts' (p. 36).

Thrasymachus: I will not 'annoy the company by contradicting you' (p. 36).

Socrates: We have established that 'just men are more intelligent and more truly effective in action', while unjust men are 'incapable of any joint action at all' (p. 36).

(iii) The just man is happier than the unjust (pp. 37–40)

Socrates: Well, it also looks as if 'the just live better and happier lives than the unjust', but let us examine the question 'more closely' (p. 37). Now, something's 'function' is 'that which only it can do or that which it does best'; and something with a function has 'its own particular excellence' (p. 38). So, eyes, for example, could not fulfil their function if, instead of their particular excellence, they had 'the corresponding defect' (p. 38).

Thrasymachus: Such as blindness?

Socrates: Or whatever it might be. In that case, they would 'perform their function badly' (p. 38). Would you agree, Thrasymachus?

Thrasymachus: Certainly.

Socrates: Would you also agree that performance of functions, such as 'paying attention, controlling, deliberating', requires the mind, and that the mind has its own 'peculiar excellence', without which it will perform its functions badly (pp. 38–9)?

Thrasymachus: It follows.

Socrates: But did we not agree that justice was 'the peculiar excellence of the mind and injustice its defect', so that the just man, with a just mind, will lead a 'good life', while the unjust man will have a bad one (p. 39)?

Thrasymachus: So it appears from your argument.

Socrates: However, the man who has a good life is 'prosperous and happy', so it is the just, not the unjust, man who is happy (p. 39). And, of course, 'it never pays to be miserable, but to be happy' (p. 39).

Thrasymachus: Enjoy your 'holiday treat', Socrates (p. 39).

Socrates: Ah, well, we still have not found the answers we were seeking. We began by asking what justice is, but broke off before we did so. As I still do not know what justice is, I am unlikely to discover 'whether it is an excellence or not, or whether it makes man happy or unhappy' (pp. 39–40).

4 Adeimantus and Glaucon Restate the Case for Injustice (pp. 40–52)

(a) Justice and morality are merely a matter of convenience (pp. 40–6)

Glaucon: I am still not convinced that right action is always 'better than wrong' (p. 41). You agree that there is a kind of good, such as **pleasure**, that we want 'for its own sake', not its **consequences**; another, such as wisdom and health, that we want 'on both grounds'; and a third, such as 'exercise and medical treatment' which, though 'painful', we choose for the 'benefits we get' (p. 41)?

Socrates: Yes.

Glaucon: Well, in which one would you put 'justice and right' (p. 41)?

Socrates: In your second and '**highest category**' (p. 41).

Glaucon: But general opinion puts it in the third. What I want to do, Socrates, is to 'revive Thrasymachus' argument' (p. 42). I shall start with the 'common opinion on the nature and origin of justice', which is that it is 'a good thing to inflict wrong or injury, and a bad thing to suffer it' (p. 42). However, as we cannot always impose the first, and ward off the second, we agree to 'forgo both' (p. 42). So, justice occupies the middle ground between what is most desirable (wrongdoing) and what is least (being the victim of it): 'not good in itself', but having the 'relative value' of preventing wrongdoing (p. 42). People would prefer to do wrong, but cannot, and so practise justice 'against their will' (p. 43). This can easily be proved. Given complete freedom, the just man will soon be caught in the same self-interested pursuits as the unjust one. No one is 'just of his own free will, but only under compulsion' (p. 44). As people always do wrong, when given the opportunity, this shows that no one thinks 'justice pays him personally' (p. 44).

As to the choice between a just and an unjust life, all will go well for an unjust man, if he can 'avoid detection in his wrongdoing', and secure a 'reputation for the highest **probity**' (p. 44). But what if a just man does not seem so, and gains a 'life-long reputation for wickedness', even though 'he has done no wrong' (p. 45)? It would be interesting to 'test his justice', and see if it fails in the face of public condemnation (p. 45). If it does not, we would be well placed to assess whether it is the just or the unjust life that brings more happiness (p. 45).

Socrates: You paint a vivid picture.

Glaucon: People would see that the just man's life is one of misery and 'humiliation', while the unjust man does well and grows rich, and they would conclude that 'a better life is provided for the unjust man than for the just by both **gods** and men' (p. 46).

(b) People do right only for what they can get out of it (pp. 46–52)

Adeimantus: The 'most essential point' has not been made (p. 46). People urge others to be just, not because they 'value' it in itself, but for 'the good reputation it brings' in this life, and for the future rewards if 'a man stands well with heaven' (p. 47). They also point to the punishment the 'unjust and irreligious' face in this life and the next (p. 47). They may commend 'the worth of self-control or justice', but they admit that they are hard to practise: unlike injustice and self-indulgence, from which more is to be gained and which are condemned 'only by **convention**' (p. 48). An unjust man is acknowledged as happy, and respected more than a just one, provided 'he is rich and powerful' (p. 48). Then there are stories about how the gods 'often allot misfortune' to the good, and how '**remission** and **absolution**' may be had through sacrifices, however great the sins (pp. 48–9). What is the point of being just when, provided we maintain a 'veneer of respectability', injustice makes it possible for us 'to do as we like with gods and men' (p. 50).

You know, Socrates, the root problem is that all the advocates of justice have never applauded it, 'except for the reputation and honours and rewards' it brings (pp. 50–1). They should have shown that 'injustice has the worst possible effect on the mind and justice the reverse', so that we would all abstain from wrongdoing out of fear of doing ourselves 'a grave and lasting injury' (p. 51). What we want from you is not only proof that justice is 'superior to injustice', but an analysis of the effects each has on the mind (p. 51). You have said that justice belongs to 'the highest category of goods' (p. 51). We want to hear you commending it for 'the real benefits it brings its possessor' (p. 51). You have made a lifetime study of this subject. Please prove to us that, whether people know it or not, justice is good, and injustice is not, because of 'its inherent effects on its possessor' (p. 52).

Part II   Preliminaries (pp. 53–66)

1   *First Principles of Social Organization (pp. 53–60)*

Socrates: It will be no easy matter to determine the nature of justice. However, as it can be 'a characteristic' of both individuals and communities, it may be easier to identify it in the 'larger entity' and, in particular, at the point when it is created (p. 55). Society comes into being because the 'individual is not self-sufficient', and has 'needs' he cannot 'supply himself' (p. 55). Also, when different people specialize in different tasks, such as farming, building or weaving, according to their 'natural aptitudes', 'quantity and quality' of production improve (pp. 56–7). And, as society develops, the number of functions will increase, to include, for example, different types of craftsmen, merchants and retailers. So, where shall we find 'justice and injustice' in this (p. 59)?

Adeimantus: Could it be in the 'mutual relationship of these elements' (p. 59)?

2   Civilized Society (pp. 60–3)

Glaucon: But the society you have described lacks the 'comforts of civilization' (p. 60).

Socrates: True, and one that has it will contain a 'multitude of occupations', from barbers to sculptors (p. 61). And, if our society does not limit itself to 'necessities', it will want to seize some of its 'neighbours' territory', and vice-versa, which will mean war and a **professional army** (p. 61). We have accepted the need for specialization, so the citizens cannot fight for themselves. Indeed, membership of the 'defence force' is so important that it demands 'complete freedom from other affairs and a correspondingly high degree of skill and practice' (pp. 62–3).

3   Qualities Required in the Guardians (pp. 63–6)

Socrates: So, our society needs a **Guardian class**, to defend and govern it. Now, are not the qualities required for Guardian-duty like those 'needed in a well-bred watch-dog', which behaves 'with the utmost gentleness to those it is used to and knows', but is 'savage to strangers' (p. 64)? The Guardian needs to be a '**philosopher**', for 'gentleness towards his own fellows and neighbours requires a **philosophic disposition** and a love of learning' (pp. 65–6).

Part III   Education: The First Stage (pp. 67–111)

1   *Secondary or Literary Education (pp. 67–100)*

(a) Current Literature Unsuitable Theologically (pp. 67–76)

Socrates: That is 'our Guardians' basic character' (p. 68). However, we must decide on their educational programme, which needs to include both mental and physical training. We shall begin with the first and, as 'fiction' will play an important part in this early stage, we must ensure that only 'suitable' stories are selected (p. 68). Many of those we use now, by '**Homer** and **Hesiod**', for example, contain the worst possible 'fault': that of 'misrepresenting the nature of gods and **heroes**' (p. 69). We cannot allow stories that show the gods fighting and plotting against each other, as that will not encourage 'excellence of character' (p. 70). God must be depicted 'as he really is': good (p. 71). Our stories must make it clear that good does not cause evil, and that '*God is the cause, not of all things, but only of good*' (p. 73). Again, the better something is, the less likely it is to be 'changed by **external influences**' so, as the gods are 'perfect in beauty and goodness', it is wrong to show them (as the poets do) appearing in 'many forms' (pp. 73–4). Further, they do not deceive, so the stories must not suggest that lies are told 'in the **realm of the spiritual and divine**' (p. 75). Plays by poets who misrepresent the gods must be banned.

Adeimantus: I agree with your principles. They must become law.

(b) Current Literature Unsuitable Morally (pp. 76–85)

Socrates: We have established what sort of stories will ensure that our future Guardians 'honour the gods and their parents', and love one another (p. 76). But, as they will be soldiers, our stories must inculcate courage and diminish fear of death, so we must exclude passages in 'Homer and the other poets', which give a 'gloomy account of the **after-life**' (p. 78). We also want plays and poems that present 'tales of endurance by famous men', as these will inspire our future Guardians (p. 83). We shall not tolerate stories in which 'unjust men are often happy, and just men wretched', or which suggest that 'wrongdoing pays' and that 'justice is what is good for someone else but is to your own disadvantage' (p. 85).

Adeimantus: Quite true.

(c) Formal Requirements of Literature (pp. 85–93)

Socrates: A story or poem contains both speeches and narrative and, when the former are read, the person doing so 'assimilates his manner of speech' as closely as possible 'to that of the character concerned', so as to '"*represent*" the person' (p. 87). It is important that, in any 'dramatic or other representations', our future Guardians, whose career will be to run the state, only act the parts of 'men of courage, self-control, piety, freedom of spirit and similar qualities' (p. 89). They must not take on the roles of cowards or other 'unworthy' characters (pp. 90–1). In general, we want to promote the work of poets who are 'severe rather than amusing', and who 'portray the style of the good man' (pp. 92–3).

Adeimantus: I agree.

(d) Musical Requirements (pp. 93–6)

Socrates: In music, we require two 'modes': one that represents 'the voice and accent of a brave man on military service', and the other that portrays him in the 'voluntary non-violent occupations of peacetime' (p. 94). Both must show his 'moderation and common sense' (p. 94).

Glaucon: Agreed.

(e) Summary (pp. 96–100)

Socrates: We are concerned with the cultivation of 'good character', so we shall instruct all our 'artists and craftsmen' not to portray 'bad character' in their work (p. 97). We do not want to see 'ill-discipline, meanness, or ugliness' (p. 97). We require artists, 'capable of perceiving the **real nature** of what is beautiful', and whose works of art influence our young people 'for good' (p. 98). For neither we, nor the future Guardians, 'whom we are training', will be 'properly educated', unless we can recognize such qualities as 'discipline, courage, generosity, greatness of mind' (p. 98).
Glaucon: Certainly.

2 Physical Education (pp. 100–11)

Socrates: In itself, 'physical excellence' does not produce 'good mind and character' (p. 101). Rather, an individual with both will 'make the best' of his physique, and will be able to deal with the 'minutiae of physical training' (p. 101). What our future Guardians require is 'simple and flexible' physical training, to make them alert and capable of enduring all the rigours that military 'campaigning entails', not that of an athlete, which can make a person highly strung and prone to 'serious illness' (pp. 101–2). They must avoid a **'luxurious' lifestyle**, as 'elaborate food produces disease' (p. 102). It is a disgrace when people need medical attention, not for disease, but because an 'idle life' has filled their 'bodies with gases and fluids, like a stagnant pool' (p. 103). And 'fussiness about one's health' is to be deplored (p. 105). We should follow **Asclepius'** approach: that it is their jobs in society that make people's lives worthwhile, so they have no time to waste on 'being ill and undergoing cures'; and there is no point in treating someone 'who cannot survive the routine of his ordinary job', as he is 'no use either to himself or society' (pp. 104–5).

Glaucon: I agree with you.

Socrates: Our state must provide for treatment of those citizens 'whose physical and psychological constitution is good' (p. 108). It will 'leave the unhealthy to die', and kill those 'whose **psychological constitution is incurably corrupt**' (p. 108).

Glaucon: That would be best for both 'the individual sufferer and society' (p. 108).

Socrates: As long as they follow our educational programme, our young men will develop 'self-control', and so never get into trouble with the law, while their physical training will ensure they never need a doctor (p. 108). Of course, the aim of both mental and physical training is to develop the mind. Those who devote themselves exclusively to one or other tend to be either 'uncivilized and tough' or 'soft and over-sensitive' (p. 109). In the Guardian, however, these elements must be 'harmoniously adjusted', so that his character is both 'self-controlled and brave' (p. 109).

Glaucon: 'That describes him exactly' (p. 110).

Socrates: So, a 'god' seems to have given us both mental and physical training to train the two parts of us: our 'philosophic part' and our 'energy and initiative' (p. 110). Their role is not to train mind and body separately, but to 'ensure a proper harmony' between 'energy and initiative on the one hand and reason on the other by tuning each to the right pitch' (p. 110). If 'its **constitution** is to be preserved', we must make sure that the person responsible for our state's education system understands all this (p. 111).

Glaucon: We 'most certainly must' (p. 111).

Part IV   Guardians and Auxiliaries (pp. 112–29)

1   *The Three Classes and Their Mutual Relations (pp. 112–17)*

Socrates: It is obvious that the 'elder' and 'best' Guardians must rule (p. 113). **Rulers** must be the most 'intelligent', and those who will 'always do what they think best for the community' (pp. 113–14). And we must monitor the progress of future Guardians from their 'earliest years', to identify those who will adhere firmly to 'this principle' (pp. 114–15). We shall need to test their integrity 'rigorously'; those who fail must be rejected (p. 115). In addition to those who govern, we shall need assistant Guardians, or '**Auxiliaries**', to help carry out decisions and serve in the army (p. 115).

You know it would be useful to have a '**magnificent myth**' about the origin of our society, which would teach all its members to accept their particular role (p. 115). It would stress the fact that all are brother members of the same community, but that, when 'god' created them, he put gold in those capable of ruling; silver in the Auxiliaries; and bronze or iron in the rest. Children will 'commonly resemble' their parents but, occasionally, 'golden parents' will have a 'silver child' and so on (p. 116). The Guardians must 'watch the mixture of metals in the character of their children', and ensure that, where necessary, children are promoted or demoted to the class (and therefore future role) for which their abilities equip them (p. 117). Do you think our citizens will believe this story?

Glaucon: Not at first, but 'second and later generations' might (p. 117).

Socrates: But it should 'increase their loyalty to the state and to each other' (p. 117).

2   *The Rulers' and Auxiliaries' Way of Life (pp. 117–21)*

Socrates: It would be appalling if our guard-dogs behaved 'like wolves', so we must ensure that our Guardians' way of life frees them from any temptation to ill-treat their fellow citizens (p. 118). In addition to their good education, they must live together in barracks, and not own any **'private property'** (p. 118). We do not want them to develop into 'harsh tyrants', as a result of being in business competition with those they exist to defend (p. 119).

Adeimantus: You are not planning a 'particularly happy' life for the Guardians. Unlike other rulers, they will not get any benefits from being in charge (p. 119).

Socrates: I think they may be 'very happy indeed' (p. 120). But our aim is not the 'happiness' of the Guardian class; it is that of the 'whole community' (p. 119). And this is most likely to occur in a well-governed state, in which there is justice.

3   *Final Provisions for Unity (pp. 121–9)*

Socrates: Wealth and poverty can ruin the non-Guardian class of society, as one leads to 'idleness', the other to 'bad workmanship' and desire for revolution; our Guardians need to prevent these occurring (p. 122).

Adeimantus: What worries me is that our state, lacking wealth, will be unable to fight off a rich and powerful enemy.

Socrates: But our **'trained soldiers'** will be equal to 'two or three times their number' (p. 123). And ours will be a united state, free of strife between rich and poor. It will be 'supreme', provided our Guardians enforce the internal 'discipline' we have outlined; do not allow the state to grow beyond the size at which a sense of unity can be sustained; and 'stick to the system of education' we have described (pp. 124–5).

Part V   Justice in State and Individual (pp. 130–56)

1   *Justice in the State (pp. 131–9)*

Socrates: So, can we identify justice in our state? As it is 'presumably perfect', it will contain the 'qualities of wisdom, courage, self-discipline, and justice' (p. 131). It is wise, as its 'judgement is good', and this is because of the 'knowledge inherent in its smallest constituent part or class', the Guardians, who exercise 'authority over the rest' (pp. 131–2). Courage is a 'sort of safe-keeping', which upholds the opinions that our education system has inculcated about what is 'to be feared', and what is correct according to our laws; and this is the quality their training has developed in 'our soldier-class' (p. 133). Self-discipline is controlling 'certain desires and appetites', as when the better element of 'the personality' controls the worse (pp. 134–5). Our state has this, and it 'stretches across' the whole community, because, with the agreement of all its members, 'the desires of the less respectable majority are controlled by the desires and wisdom of the superior minority' (pp. 135–6). And now I see what justice is.
Glaucon: Good.
Socrates: It is the idea that, in our state, one man does one job, the job he is 'naturally most suited for' (p. 137). Our state is just when 'each of our **three classes (businessmen**, Auxiliaries and Guardians) does its own job and minds its own business', making it the quality that contributes most to our state's 'excellence' (pp. 138–9).

2   *The Elements in Mental Conflict (pp. 139–49)*

Socrates: Now with the individual, we would expect to find that there are '**three elements in his personality**', corresponding to the three classes in our state (p. 142). And this is the case. Obviously, there is a 'reflective element in the mind', the **reason**, and that which 'feels hunger and thirst, and the agitations of sex and other desires, the element of **irrational appetite**' (p. 147). But is there a third, which we might call, '**indignation**' (p. 147)?

Glaucon: That sounds like appetite.

Socrates: But think of the man who is furious with himself, because his desires are trying to make him do something of which 'his reason disapproves' (p. 148). Does indignation ever side with desires against the 'decision of reason' (p. 148)? Surely, indignation is 'reason's natural auxiliary' (p. 149).

Glaucon: Quite right.

3 Justice in the Individual (pp. 149–54)

Socrates: We agreed that 'the state was just when the three elements within it each minded their own business' (p. 150). Thus, in the individual, 'the reason ought to rule, having the wisdom and foresight to act for the whole', while the spirit 'ought to obey and support it' (p. 150). The 'combination of intellectual and physical training' we have described will develop this 'concord'; and these two elements, working together, will control the 'insatiable' appetite (pp. 150–1). And when there is no 'civil war' among these elements, and reason rules, do we not call the individual concerned, 'self-disciplined' (p. 151)? So, justice in the individual is like that in the state. The just man will not permit 'the three elements which make up his inward self to trespass on each other's functions' (p. 152). In the same way that health results from 'a natural relation of control and subordination' among parts of the body, justice results from 'establishing in the mind a similar natural relation of control and subordination among its constituents' (p. 154).

Glaucon: Very true.

4   Conclusion *(pp. 154–6)*

Socrates: Finally, does it pay to 'act justly and behave honourably' (p. 154)?

Glaucon: Our discussion has made it an absurd 'question' (p. 155). A man's life is not 'worth living' if he chooses to avoid acquiring 'justice and excellence' (p. 155).

Socrates: Nevertheless, it would be instructive to enumerate the 'different forms of wickedness' (p. 155). I think we shall find that there are 'as many types of character as there are types and forms of political constitution': five, one good and four bad (p. 155). Our constitution, the 'good and true' one, can be called either 'a **Monarchy**', if there is one 'outstanding' ruler, or 'an **Aristocracy**'; but the crucial requirement is that the rulers have been educated 'as we have described' (pp. 155–6).

Part VI   Women and the Family *(pp. 157–88)*

1   *The Status of Women (pp. 157–67)*

Adeimantus: What will the Guardians' family life be like? How are they to 'produce children, and bring them up' (p. 158)?

Socrates: Should 'female watchdogs' have the same duties as male ones (p. 160)?

Glaucon: The same.

Socrates: If we apply this to women, we shall have to 'teach them the same things' as men (p. 161). But, given the 'natural differences' between men and women, it is debatable whether women are 'naturally capable of taking part in all the occupations of the male', or of any (p. 162). However, we need to identify the kind of 'difference of nature we mean' (p. 163). We are not talking about differences in an 'unqualified sense', but of those that are 'relevant to various employments', and the fact that men beget, and women bear, children is not a relevant consideration (p. 164). The relevant factors are intellectual ability and physical co-ordination, so there is no '**administrative occupation**' that is peculiarly suited to either men or women, any more than to bald or 'long-haired men' (pp. 164–5). Rather, '**natural capacities** are similarly distributed in each sex, and it is natural for women to take part in all occupations as well as men' (p. 165). Although they will tend to be 'the weaker partners', there are women capable of 'soldiering', doing philosophy and of being Guardians (pp. 165–6). These must have the same 'intellectual and physical training' as their male counterparts and, just as the Guardians, as a class, will be 'the best citizens', the female Guardians will be 'the best women' (pp. 166–7).

2 *Marriage and the Family (pp. 167–82)*

Socrates: What is more, our male and female Guardians must not be allowed to 'live together in separate households' (p. 168). Both women and children should be held in common, so that neither parents nor children know each other.
Glaucon: This idea will encounter 'scepticism' (p. 168).
Socrates: Even so, it is essential. All our Guardians must live together and own 'no private home or property' (p. 169). Further, we must bring together male and female Guardians of 'similar natural capacities', mating the 'best' men and women often, but the 'inferior' ones infrequently, and bringing up 'only the offspring of the best' (pp. 169–71). This is the way to ensure 'a **real pedigree herd**' (p. 171). All this will require careful management by 'the Rulers', who alone will have full knowledge of the arrangements (p. 171). They must institute '**sacred**' marriage festivals, which will include 'religious sacrifices' and appropriate poetry (pp. 170–1). They will decide the

number of unions, with the aim of **keeping 'numbers constant', and maintaining the size of the state**; and they will need to 'devise an ingenious system of drawing lots', to prevent the 'inferior Guardians' realizing what is going on (p. 171). Specially appointed officers will remove the 'children of the better Guardians to a nursery'; those of '**inferior Guardians**' and any '**defective offspring**' will be 'quietly and secretly disposed of' (pp. 171–2).

Glaucon: I see.

Socrates: We must also ensure that we 'breed from creatures in their prime' (p. 172). Women should 'bear **children for the state**' between the ages of 20 and 40; men from 25 to 55 (p. 172). If those above or below these ages try to beget 'children for the community', it will be treated as a 'sin and a crime' (p. 172). Also, if those within these age ranges produce a child without the Rulers' consent, it will be treated as 'a bastard on both civil and religious grounds' (pp. 172–3). Those over the breeding age can mate freely, provided they do not do so with their children, grandchildren, parents or antecedents. But they must prevent the birth of any conception from such relationships, or otherwise '**dispose of it as a creature that must not be reared**' (p. 173).

Glaucon: Well and good, but how will they know who their relatives are?

Socrates: They cannot. However, a man will regard all the children born within ten months of his being a bridegroom as his sons and daughters, and their children as his grandchildren; and they will call 'his marriage-group' their fathers or grandfathers; and so on (p. 173). Thus, they will '**observe the prohibitions we mentioned**' (p. 173).

Glaucon: Of course.

Socrates: So, why is all this necessary? The worst thing for a state is to be 'split and fragmented'; the best for it to have 'cohesion and unity' (p. 176). In a well-ordered state, people 'use the words "mine" and "not mine" in the same sense of the same things' (pp. 176–7). In our state, both 'rulers and common' people will call each other '**fellow-citizens**'; the ordinary people will regard their rulers as 'protectors and defenders'; and the rulers will be united by their being each other's brothers, sisters, fathers and mothers (pp. 177–8). Unlike the rulers of other states, they will be '**devoted to a common interest**', and the 'community of women and children' will prevent 'the dissension' that arises when rulers accumulate wealth for themselves, or promote their own family interests (p. 178–9). Our laws 'will mean that the Guardians will live at complete peace with each other' (p. 180). Do you agree, then, that 'the best arrangement is for our men and women to share a common education, to bring up their children in common, and to have a common responsibility, as Guardians, for their fellow-citizens' (p. 181)?

Glaucon: I agree.

3 The Rules of War (pp. 182–8)

Socrates: In war, men and women 'will serve together', and take their children with them, to see the job they will do when they grow up (p. 182). Cowards and deserters will be 'relegated to the **artisans** or farmers'; those who show great courage will be honoured on the spot by their fellow-campaigners, and this will be followed by sacrifices and feasts; while those who die bravely in battle will be reckoned 'men of gold', and buried with 'special ceremonies' (pp. 184–5).

Glaucon: 'Very right' (p. 185).

Socrates: As to treatment of the enemy, it is **wrong to sell other Greeks into slavery**. It is better to spare them, if only through fear of all of us 'falling under **barbarian** domination' (p. 185).

Glaucon: We must 'let each other alone and turn against the barbarian' (p. 186).

Socrates: And we must not plunder the corpses, or devastate the lands, of other Greeks. In fact, we should insist that we fight wars only against the barbarians, who are our natural enemies. Greek fighting Greek is '"civil strife"', due to Greece being 'sick and torn by faction' (p. 187). The people of our state 'will love their fellow-Greeks, and think of Greece as their own land, in whose common religion they share' (p. 187).

Part VII   The Philosopher Ruler (pp. 189–248)

1   *The Ideal and the Actual (pp. 189–92)*

Glaucon: But, Socrates, although the state you have described would be 'ideal if it existed', you need to prove that it can exist (p. 189).

Socrates: When I do, you will see why I hesitate to put forward 'such a **paradoxical theory**' (p. 190). We are considering the nature of justice and injustice. Now, 'when we find out what justice is', shall we be satisfied with an approximation to it (p. 190)?

Glaucon: Yes.

Socrates: We want to pinpoint what the 'perfectly just' is like, rather than 'show that the ideal could be realized in practice' (p. 190)?

Glaucon: True.

Socrates: We would not object if a painter could not show that the 'ideally beautiful man' in his picture actually existed (p. 190).

Glaucon: No.

Socrates: So, our 'word-picture of an **ideal state**' will be none the worse if its actual existence cannot be shown (pp. 190–1)?

And you agree, given the gap there always is between theory and practice, that I need only indicate the 'conditions' under which a state could 'most closely approximate' to the ideal (p. 191)?

Glaucon: Yes.

Socrates: Well, you may laugh, but the 'troubles' of 'existing states' (and of humanity) will not end until **philosophers become kings in this world**', or at least, our present rulers become philosophers (pp. 191–2).

Glaucon: You will have your work cut out defending this pronouncement, but I shall give you all the help I can (p. 192).

2   *Definition of the Philosopher (pp. 192–208)*

(a) *The Philosopher and the Two Orders of Reality*
(pp. 192–204)

Socrates: First, we must 'define these philosophers', to show they are equipped for 'philosophy and political leadership' (p. 196). If a man loves something, he loves the whole of it; he wants 'everything of that particular kind' (pp. 196–7). Thus, the philosopher's passion is for 'wisdom of every kind' (p. 197). His thirst for 'every branch of learning' is never satisfied (p. 197).

Glaucon: That covers a lot of 'peculiar people', such as those interested in the 'minor arts' (pp. 197–8).

Socrates: To be precise, philosophers 'love to see the **truth**' (p. 198). Many people like to look at beautiful things, and may be able to recognize beautiful objects individually, but are unable to perceive 'the **essential nature of beauty itself**' (p. 198). But what about the man who believes in beauty itself, sees both it and the things that share it, and does not confuse the latter with 'that in which they share' (p. 199)?

Glaucon: He is in a fortunate position.

Socrates: He has **'knowledge', while the others have only 'opinions'** (p. 199). What about those with opinions? Do they know 'something or nothing' (p. 199)?

Glaucon: 'Something' (p. 199).

Socrates: Thus, what 'fully *is* is fully knowable', and what is not is 'entirely unknowable' (p. 199)? And anything that both is and is not would lie in between, and 'something *between* ignorance and knowledge' would relate to it (p. 199). Now, is not 'opinion' different from knowledge' (p. 200)?

Glaucon: Yes.

Socrates: We have 'faculties', like sight and hearing, which, as they are not tangible, can be identified only by their 'field and effects' (p. 200). Is knowledge a faculty?

Glaucon: The 'most powerful' (p. 200).

Socrates: And opinion, given that it is not the same as knowledge?

Glaucon: A different faculty.

Socrates: Knowledge is concerned with 'what is', but do knowledge and opinion have the same fields (p. 201)?

Glaucon: Different ones.

Socrates: Which must be something 'other than what is' (p. 201)?

Glaucon: Yes.

Socrates: We have correlated 'ignorance with *what is not*, knowledge with *what is*'; but an opinion must relate to something, rather than nothing (p. 201). It is 'darker than knowledge, but clearer than ignorance', and is 'intermediate between them' (p. 202). Therefore, we need to find the **'object of opinion'**, which will share both **'being and non-being'** (p. 202). So, let us return to those who love beautiful things, but deny 'beauty in itself or any eternally unchanging **form of beauty'**, and the same with justice and so on (p. 202). What if we ask them whether there is a beautiful object, or a 'just and righteous' act, that does not also seem ugly or unjust (p. 202)?

Glaucon: They will all seem both.

Socrates: Can we say that any of these things '*is*', any more than it '*is not*' (p. 203)?

Glaucon: They cannot be thought of as either 'being' or 'not-being' (p. 203).

Socrates: Thus, 'many conventional views' about beauty and so on lie between 'what is not and what fully is' (p. 203). And we agreed previously that anything like this should be considered 'the field of opinion', not knowledge (p. 203).

Glaucon: Yes.

Socrates: Those who see beautiful objects or just acts, but not beauty or justice themselves, can be said to have '*opinions*' about, but not knowledge of, them (p. 203). But the reverse is the case with those who see '**eternal, unchanging things**' (p. 203).

Glaucon: Agreed.

Socrates: And we will be entitled to call them 'lovers of opinion', rather than wisdom, for only those 'whose hearts are fixed on the true being of each thing' can be called 'philosophers' (p. 204).

Glaucon: Quite right.

(b) The Qualities of Character Required in the Philosopher (pp. 204–8)

Socrates: We can now see, Glaucon, what a philosopher is. So, if the philosopher can 'grasp the eternal and **immutable**', while others are immersed in '**multiplicity and change**', who should rule the state (p. 204)?

Glaucon: What do you think?

Socrates: Our Guardians must be those who can 'guard the **laws and customs of society**' (p. 204). In the same way that a blind man makes a poor guard, it would be folly to have as rulers those who are blind to 'reality', and who have '**no clear standard' of right and good** on which to base the rules they impose (pp. 204–5).

Glaucon: Then, we should choose philosophers, provided they possess all the necessary qualities.

Socrates: A philosopher loves any part of learning that 'reveals **eternal reality**' (p. 205). Thus, he will love truth and hate untruth, as nothing is closer to 'wisdom than truth' (p. 206). However, a man who is strongly inclined 'in one direction' (in this case towards the mind) may be less strongly inclined in another (p. 206). He will be indifferent to physical pleasures and money, and will not be petty-minded, as this is incompatible with trying to 'grasp things divine or human as a whole' (p. 206). He will not fear death, and, being neither 'cowardly' nor 'ungenerous', he will not be 'unjust' or uncivilized (p. 207). He will learn easily, and have a good memory and a 'sense of proportion', which will lead him on 'to see the form of each reality' (p. 207). Can any fault be found with an occupation that requires 'good memory, readiness to learn, breadth of vision and grace . . . truth, justice, courage, and self-control' (p. 208)?

Glaucon: Certainly not.

Socrates: Then these are the ones 'to whom you would entrust your state' (p. 208).

3 The Prejudice Against Philosophy and the Corruption of the Philosophic Nature in Contemporary Society (pp. 208–19)

Adeimantus: That sounds fine, Socrates, but your arguments are like a 'game of draughts': the expert player always wins (p. 209). It was difficult to find a point at which to contradict you but, in reality, those who devote their lives to philosophy seem pretty useless to society.

Socrates: A fair point, so let me give an 'illustration', to show how hard it is for 'the better type of philosopher in contemporary society' (pp. 209–10). Imagine a ship with a 'deaf and short-sighted' captain, whose 'seamanship' is poor (p. 210). The crew members know nothing of navigation, but jostle the captain, trying to get the helm. In the end, one who can successfully manipulate the captain takes control. Now this crew would not recognize a professional navigator if one came aboard, and would probably dismiss him as a 'word-spinner and a star-gazer' (p. 210). This is society's attitude to the 'true philosopher' (p. 210).

Adeimantus: I see.

Socrates: Do not blame the philosophers for society's failure to make use of them. Those in need of direction should wait on 'him who can give it', but this is not the way it is, even though our present politicians are, like the sailors, not 'true navigators' (p. 211).

Adeimantus: True.

Socrates: Even more 'damaging' is the effect of those who 'pretend' to practise philosophy; they really are 'useless' (p. 211). But it is not philosophy's fault that most philosophers are 'corrupted' (p. 211). Remember, a true philosopher must pursue truth 'at all costs' (p. 211). Not satisfied with what 'opinion takes for reality', he must grasp 'the nature of each thing as it is' (p. 212). You would agree that such a man hates 'falsehood' (p. 212)?

Adeimantus: Agreed.

Socrates: Such a man is just, of 'sound character' and self-disciplined (p. 212). So, why does the 'philosophic nature' deteriorate (p. 212)?

Adeimantus: Go on.

Socrates: The qualities of the 'ideal philosopher' occur rarely (p. 213). Curiously enough, it is their praiseworthy qualities, together with the **'good things of life'**, such as 'wealth', which corrupt them, and lure them away from philosophy (p. 212). You know also that if a seed is put in the wrong environment, it will not grow properly?

Adeimantus: Yes.

Socrates: Now 'high natural quality' fares less well in a bad environment than 'poor quality', so the 'most gifted characters' become 'particularly bad', if their upbringing is unsatisfactory (pp. 213–14). The philosophic nature will only 'develop every excellence' under the right conditions (p. 214). And just think how 'the public' behaves in 'the **assembly** or **law courts**', yelling approval or disapproval of what takes place (p. 214). Young men are overwhelmed by this torrent of 'popular praise and blame', and adopt 'popular ideas of what is admirable or disgraceful' (p. 214). In today's society, it is impossible to develop excellence of character on lines that differ from generally accepted standards.

Adeimantus: You are right.

Socrates: And look at the teachers, who put across the 'conventional views' of **the masses** (p. 215). Imagine someone in charge of a 'large and powerful animal' (p. 215). He studies and learns its moods, so that he knows how to manage it from its reactions. He describes this as a science, and starts to teach it. But he does not know which of its 'tastes and desires' are 'good or bad, right or wrong'; rather, he calls what pleases it good and what provokes it bad (p. 215). What sort of teacher is he?

Adeimantus: A poor one.

Socrates: But how does such a teacher differ from one who regards knowledge of the **'passions and pleasures' of the masses** as science, and who sets out to win their approval (pp. 215–16). Do you think that the mass of humanity can distinguish between what something, such as beauty, 'is in itself' and examples of it (p. 216)?

Adeimantus: No.

Socrates: Therefore, philosophy is 'impossible' among the masses, who will 'disapprove of philosophers', as will those who curry favour with the masses (p. 216). In this environment, the potential philosopher will be unable to persevere with his 'vocation' (p. 216). Society will take up a man who shows promise, and cultivate and flatter him, in order to use him for its 'own purposes' (p. 216). And what will be the result, particularly if he is a citizen of a great country, and wealthy and good-looking? Inevitably, his ambition will be fired and, full of pride and self-confidence, he will believe himself 'capable of running the affairs of Greece' (pp. 216–17). And, if somebody tells him that he still has much to learn, he is unlikely to listen.

Adeimantus: Indeed not.

Socrates: But, if his 'natural gifts' still incline him to philosophy, his companions will do their utmost to dissuade him (p. 217). So, 'many influences' exist to 'destroy the best natures', and distract them from the 'highest' pursuit (p. 217). And, whereas they could have done a lot of good in their societies, they may, because of their great gifts, inflict tremendous harm. Then, with the best minds deserting philosophy, 'second-rate interlopers' take it up and devalue it (p. 218). Those who are unsuited for philosophy produce ideas that lack 'any trace of true wisdom' (p. 218). Of course, there are some who, having 'tasted the happiness of philosophy and seen the frenzy of the masses', recognize that political life has nothing to offer, as they will lack support in any 'fight for justice' (p. 219). Refusing to join in the general wickedness, they withdraw from society, and 'live quietly' (p. 219).

Adeimantus: No small achievement.

Socrates: But how much better it would be if society encouraged them to 'develop more fully', for their benefit and its own (p. 219).

4 The Philosopher Ruler Is Not Impossible (pp. 219–25)

Socrates: Existing forms of society do not suit the 'philosophic nature', and so it 'degenerates' (p. 220). The state needs to 'tackle philosophy' in a way 'quite opposite' to its 'present' approach (p. 220). Currently, young men study it for a time, and then give it up when they have barely scratched its surface.

Adeimantus: What is the right way?

Socrates: The young should do a limited amount of philosophy, and their 'mental training' should increase as they get older (p. 221). When their minds are mature, they can give 'their main energies to philosophy' (p. 21). There will never be a perfect society or individuals, until the 'minority of uncorrupted philosophers' are forced to engage in politics (p. 222).

Adeimantus: I agree, but most will not.

Socrates: You are too pessimistic. We must show people what we 'mean by philosophers' (p. 222). Popular prejudice against philosophy arises from the bad impression made by current practitioners. The minds of true philosophers are focused on the **'immutable realities'**, where all is order and reason and there is no injustice (p. 223). They will endeavour to introduce the standards of the **'divine order'** into society (p. 223). Of course, they will need to 'wipe the slate of human society and human habits clean', so that they can develop the outline of the new **'social system'** (pp. 223–4). They will study 'justice and beauty and self-discipline' in their 'true nature', and then the copy of these they are trying to make in 'human beings'

(p. 224). The aim will be to make human nature 'as acceptable to God as may be' (p. 224). Do you think that critics of our theory that society's troubles will only end if philosophers control it might now come round to the idea?

Adeimantus: If they have any sense.

Socrates: We only need one such philosopher. Once he has power, and establishes 'all the laws and customs we have described', there is no reason to think that the citizens will disobey them (p. 225).

Adeimantus: Indeed not.

Socrates: So our 'proposed **legislation**' would be the ideal and not 'impossible' to introduce (p. 225).

5   *The Good as Ultimate Object of Knowledge (pp. 226–35)*

(a) The Qualities of Character the Philosopher Must Have (pp. 226–31)

Socrates: So, which studies will 'produce these saviours of our society' (p. 226)? They must 'love their country', and we need to test 'their loyalty' thoroughly, to ensure that they are fit to be rulers (p. 226). They must be philosophers 'in the fullest sense' (p. 227). We will not easily find such diverse qualities as 'quickness and keenness of mind', on the one hand, and steadiness and reliability, on the other, in the same individuals; but both are essential (p. 227).

Adeimantus: Indeed so.

Socrates: Our future leaders must be able 'to reach the **highest form of knowledge**' (p. 228).

Adeimantus: Yes, but what is it?

Socrates: Knowledge of 'the **form of the good**, from which things that are just and so on derive their usefulness and value' (p. 229). We have insufficient knowledge of it but, without it, we cannot benefit from other knowledge, because we are ignorant of 'what is good and valuable' (p. 229). While 'ordinary people' consider pleasure is the good, 'more sophisticated' ones believe it is knowledge (p. 229). However, being unsure what knowledge is, they say 'knowledge of the good' (p. 229). Then they talk as if we should know what it is, and understand what is meant by 'the word "good"' (p. 229).

Adeimantus: Very true.

Socrates: What about those who 'define good as pleasure' (p. 229)? As there are '**bad pleasures**', they have to admit that 'the same things are both good and bad' (p. 229).

Adeimantus: Yes.

Socrates: With 'justice or value', people may prefer the 'appearance to the reality', but they want something that *'really* is' good (pp. 229–31). It is the 'end of all endeavour', and a 'Guardian of what is right and valuable' must know 'in what their goodness consists' (p. 230).

Glaucon: Yes, Socrates, but what is the good?

Socrates: Have you noticed that having a '**true opinion** without understanding' is like being a 'blind man on the right road' (p. 230)? I would be in the same position if I tried to say 'what the good is in itself' (p. 231). But I will tell you about something that resembles it 'very closely' (p. 231).

Glaucon: Go on.

(b) The Simile of the Sun (pp. 231–5)

Socrates: We distinguish '**particular**' **beautiful and good things** from the **single forms of beauty and goodness**, which is what each of them '"really is"' (p. 232). Whereas the particulars are visible, the forms are '**objects of intelligence**' (p. 232).

Glaucon: Certainly.

Socrates: We see with sight, hear with hearing, and so on, but one sense requires a further 'element', in order to function (p. 232). We cannot see, unless there is light, which is provided by the **sun**.

Glaucon: True.

Socrates: The sun is not 'identical with sight', nor with the eye; rather, the eye's ability to see is a '**kind of infusion** dispensed to it by the sun' (p. 233). It causes sight, and is also seen by it. The good's relation to 'intelligence and intelligible objects in the intelligible realm' is like the sun's to 'sight and visible objects in the visible realm' (p. 233). When the mind focuses on 'objects illuminated by truth and reality', it can know and understand them (p. 234) But, in the '**twilight world of change and decay**', it can only 'form opinions' about things (p. 234). And what provides both objects of knowledge with their truth, and individuals with their 'power of knowing', is the 'form of the good' (p. 234). But, of course, while knowledge and truth are like the good, they are not the good itself, which is 'ranked still higher' (p. 234).

Glaucon: I see.

Socrates: Going back to our sun **simile**, it not only makes things visible, it causes them to grow. Similarly, the good gives objects of knowledge both their intelligibility and their 'reality', although it exceeds that reality in 'dignity and power' (p. 234).

6 *The Analogy of the Divided Line (pp. 235–40)*

Socrates: Keep in mind these '**two orders of things, the visible and the intelligible**', with 'these two powers' supreme over them (p. 237). Then, think of a line, divided into 'two unequal parts', which is again divided 'in the same ratio' (p. 238). For the 'visible order', this gives a sub-section of '"**images**"' (D), such as shadows and reflections, while (C) is for 'the originals of the images', such as animals and plants (p. 238). Is the difference between them that one is 'genuine', the other not, and that the relation of 'image to original' is that of 'the realm of opinion to that of knowledge' (p. 238)?

Glaucon: Indeed.

Socrates: In sub-section (B) of the 'intelligible part of the line', the mind 'uses the originals of the **visible order**' as 'images', and bases 'its inquiries on **assumptions**', moving from them to a 'conclusion', not a '**first principle**' (p. 238). In (A), it goes from 'assumption to a first principle' without the use of images, proceeding 'solely by and through forms themselves' (p. 238). Let me illustrate the point. Those studying geometry make certain 'basic assumptions' about 'geometrical figures', and then move by 'consistent steps' to their conclusion (p. 238). They use 'visible figures', but their concern is not really with them, but with the 'originals' they resemble, which are 'invisible except to the eye of reason' (p. 239).

Glaucon: True.

Socrates: I referred to 'this type of thing' as 'intelligible', but acknowledged that the mind had to 'use assumptions in investigating it' (p. 239). It uses the objects in (C), which have images in (D), and so cannot 'rise above its assumptions' and 'proceed to a first principle' (p. 239). However, by the 'other sub-section of the intelligible part of the line', I mean that which the 'process of argument grasps by the power of **dialectic**' (p. 239). Here assumptions are not '**principles**', but 'starting points', from which to ascend to something that 'involves no assumption and is the first principle of everything' (p. 239). That 'grasped', the mind can 'descend' to a conclusion (p. 239). This process 'moves solely through forms to forms', and does not involve 'the **sensible world**' (p. 239).

Glaucon: You wish to establish that 'part (A) of the real and intelligible (A+B)', which is studied by 'dialectic', is much clearer than (B), which is studied by the sciences, because, although they use reason, not '**sense-perception**', in dealing with their subject-matter, they regard 'assumptions as first principles', and move '*from*' them, rather than '*to* a first principle' (pp. 239–40). They do not 'exercise intelligence on it', although a 'first principle' would make it 'intelligible' (p. 240). You would describe what geometers do as 'reason but not intelligence', and as lying between 'opinion (C+D) and intelligence (A)' (p. 240).

Socrates: Precisely. There are '**four states of mind**', corresponding to the '**four sections of the line**': 'intelligence', 'reason', '**belief**' and '**illusion**'; and their 'degree of clarity' is in proportion to their subject-matter's 'degree of truth' (p. 240).

7 The Simile of the Cave (pp. 240–8)

Socrates: Think of the 'enlightenment or ignorance of our human condition' thus (p. 241). There is a cave-like 'underground chamber', with a long entrance open to daylight (p. 241). It contains men, imprisoned from childhood, so bound that they cannot turn their heads (p. 241). Behind and above them burns a fire and, between it and them, there is a road (also above them), in front of which is a 'curtain-wall', like the screen above which puppeteers display their puppets (p. 241). Now, imagine people carrying all sorts of different objects, which show above the screen, along the road. Would the prisoners see anything of people or objects, apart from the 'shadows', projected on to the wall of the cave opposite them (p. 241)?

Glaucon: No.

Socrates: Would they regard the shadows as 'real things', and think any voices belonged to the shadows (p. 241)?

Glaucon: Yes.

Socrates: Imagine a released prisoner turning towards the fire. Too 'dazzled' to see the real objects properly, he would think that the shadows he saw previously were 'nearer reality', and would want to 'retreat' to them (p. 242). If forced 'into the sunlight' of the '**upper world**', would he be able to see any of the things 'he was now told were real' (p. 242)?

Glaucon: He would not.

Socrates: He would have to adjust gradually, looking first at shadows and reflections, before he could 'look directly' at the sun, 'as it is in itself' (pp. 242–3). But, in the end, he would realize that it 'controls everything in the visible world' (p. 243). Then, he would not want to return to his previous opinions and, if he did revisit the cave, having left the sunlight, would he be 'blinded by the darkness' (p. 243)?

Glaucon: Certainly.

Socrates: If he tried to identify the different shadows, before his eyes acclimatized to darkness, he would 'make a fool of himself' (p. 243). His former companions would say that his time in the upper world had 'ruined his sight' (p. 243). So, let us connect the 'simile' with what we have said before. The prison is the 'realm revealed by sight', and the light of the fire is the 'power of the sun' (p. 244). The 'ascent into the upper world' is the mind's 'upward progress' to the 'intelligible region', and the last thing to be seen there is 'the form of the good' (p. 244). Those who have seen it will **infer** its responsibility for light and the source of light in the visible world, and for 'truth and intelligence' in the intelligible one (p. 244). Familiarity with it is essential for rational action in either 'public or private life' (p. 244).

Glaucon: Accepted.

Socrates: Now you see why those who have seen it prefer to stay in 'the realm above', rather than immerse themselves in 'human affairs'; and also why such people may show mental confusion, and find it difficult to discuss what is just with those who 'have never seen justice itself' (p. 244)?

Glaucon: Indeed.

Socrates: We must dismiss educational theories that claim to insert into the mind 'knowledge that was not there before' (p. 245). The 'capacity for knowledge' is **innate**, and the mind must be 'turned away from the **world of change**', until it can look directly at 'reality' and its 'brightest' part: 'the good' (p. 245).

Glaucon: I understand.

Socrates: Society cannot be ruled well by the 'uneducated', who know nothing of 'the truth', or 'intellectuals', who refuse to involve themselves in 'practical action' (p. 246). Our task, as 'lawgivers', is to get the 'best minds' to attain the '**vision of the good**', but to prevent them from staying in 'the upper world' and refusing to engage in the affairs of society (p. 246).

Glaucon: But they will then lead a 'poorer life' (p. 246).

Socrates: The 'object of our legislation' is not to secure the well-being of one particular group, but of 'society as a whole' (pp. 246–7). All must contribute to the general welfare, and be a 'link in the unity of the whole' (p. 247).

Glaucon: Yes, of course.

Socrates: We can tell our philosophers that, in other states, they would not have to engage in politics; but those states do not train their philosophers. We have trained ours as political leaders, for the benefit of 'the whole community' (p. 247). Knowing the truth about the just and the good, they can distinguish between the various 'shadows', and know what they are shadows of, while their lack of 'enthusiasm' for government fits them to rule (p. 247). Can they then refuse to play their part?

Glaucon: They cannot.

Socrates: Rulers seeking personal rewards from politics pursue 'rivals' quarrels', and create 'internal and domestic conflicts' (p. 248). The 'Guardians of our state' must be men who do not love power; who would prefer to be doing something else; and who attach most value to 'a good and rational life' (p. 248). Thus, a 'well-governed state' is only possible when the rulers are practitioners of 'true philosophy' (p. 248).

Glaucon: How right you are.

Part VIII   The Education of the Philosopher (pp. 249–74)

1   *Preliminary (pp. 249–54)*

Socrates: But how are we to create our philosophers and rulers? As in our story, we need to convert their minds 'from a kind of twilight to the true day', so that they ascend into the reality of true philosophy (pp. 249–50). We need to identify studies that will move their minds from 'the world of change to reality' (p. 250).

Glaucon: Indeed.

Socrates: And I think that number and counting have 'great power to draw men to reality' (p. 251).

2   *The Five Mathematical Studies (pp. 254–63)*

(a) Arithmetic (pp. 254–6)

Socrates: You see 'our perception of the **unit**' is combined with perception of its opposite, and so involves '**plurality** as much as unity'; we see 'the same thing both as a unit and as an **unlimited plurality**' (p. 254). It requires the 'exercise of judgement', and therefore, it, and 'number as a whole', will 'lead the mind on towards truth' (pp. 254–5). So, our future

Guardians will study number, not for 'commercial ends', but so that they can 'understand, by pure thought, the nature of numbers' (p. 255).

(b) Plane Geometry (pp. 256–8)

Socrates: Now, can study of geometry make it 'easier to see the form of the good' (pp. 256–7)?

Glaucon: It will only be useful if 'it compels us to contemplate reality rather than the **realm of change**' (p. 257).

Socrates: Indeed. And there is no doubt that 'the objects of geometrical knowledge are eternal', and so it will 'direct the philosophers' reason upwards' (p. 257). Further, it has uses in war.

(c) Solid Geometry (pp. 258–59)

Socrates: Next, we should include solid geometry, the study of '**cubes** and other three-dimensional figures' (p. 258). At present, it is a rather neglected subject, but it has great value, and more progress could be made in it 'under state encouragement' (p. 259).

(d) Astronomy (pp. 259–61)

Glaucon: Obviously, astronomy must be included, because it 'compels the mind to look upwards and leads it from earth to the heavens' (p. 260).

Socrates: I am afraid I do not accept that the mind looks upwards, 'except by studying the real and the invisible' (p. 260). Mere star-gazing engages the eyes, not the mind. The stars may be the 'finest and most perfect' things we can see but, for this reason, are 'far inferior' to the 'true realities' (p. 260). We shall 'ignore the visible heavens', and regard astronomy as 'setting us problems for solution' (p. 261).

(e) Harmonics (pp. 262–3)

Socrates: We shall treat this like astronomy: our pupils will not waste 'their time on measuring **audible concords** and notes against each other' (p. 262).

3 Dialectic (pp. 263–7)

Socrates: Pursuing these studies, until 'their common ground and relationship' is seen, will be a beginning (p. 263). But we want our pupils (and this is 'the exercise of dialectic'), by 'relying on reason without any aid from the senses', to move out from 'the shadows', and to persevere, until they have 'grasped by pure thought what the good is in itself', and thus reached 'the summit of the intellectual realm' (p. 264). Only 'the power of dialectic' can (for those who have followed our prescribed course of studies) lead 'the best element in the mind up towards the vision of the best among realities' (p. 264). It can do so, because it alone destroys 'assumptions', and proceeds to 'the **very first principle**' (p. 265). Indeed, we should invent a new name for the subjects we have previously classed as knowledge because, although they have more 'clarity than opinion', they are not knowledge (p. 265).

Glaucon: I agree, 'so far as I can follow you' (p. 266).

Socrates: A '**dialectician**' is able to 'take account of the **essential nature of each thing**' (p. 266). And this applies to 'the good' (p. 266). If someone cannot 'define the form of the good', and distinguish it from other things, he does not know what the good is 'in itself', nor can he identify things that are good (p. 266). All he may have is opinion, not knowledge. As it enables our pupils to gain this all-important knowledge, dialectic is 'the coping-stone that tops our educational system' (p. 267).

4 *Selection and Curriculum (pp. 267–74)*

Socrates: We shall select, for this long course of study, those with a 'natural aptitude' for it, who are eager to learn, brave, and who possess 'moral integrity and toughness' (p. 268). They should start 'arithmetic and geometry and all the other studies leading to dialectic' when children (p. 269). It is also important that there is no 'compulsion in our teaching' (p. 269).

Glaucon: Why not?

Socrates: Things taught by compulsion do not stick in the mind; lessons should 'take the form of play' (p. 270). Our pupils must have 'necessary physical training', performance in which will be an indicator of progress (p. 270). We shall choose some for promotion at 20, when they will need to bring together 'the disconnected subjects' they have studied, and take a 'comprehensive view' of their relationship to each other and 'the nature of reality' (p. 270). A further selection, at 30, will be of those whose 'perseverance' shows their 'ability to follow truth into the realm of pure reality', without the aid of the senses (p. 270). This will be 'tested by the power of dialectic'; but we need to approach dialectic with caution (p. 270).

Glaucon: Why so?

Socrates: Just look at the 'appalling harm' it does now (p. 271). People learn **conventional opinions** about 'what is right and honourable' from their parents, and repeat these opinions, when questioned about the subject (p. 271). But, when these views are 'refuted in argument', they come to believe that there is no difference between what is 'honourable and disgraceful', or 'right and good' (p, 272).

Glaucon: So they 'show less respect' (p. 272).

Socrates: Yes. They lose respect for their 'former beliefs', without having 'found the truth' (p. 272). It is the result of people starting philosophy when they are too young. They become addicted to argument and cross-examination and, after proving others wrong, and being proved wrong themselves, conclude that 'nothing they believed before was true': which tends to 'discredit' philosophy (pp. 272–3). We must ensure that only men of 'steady and disciplined character' study philosophy, as they will be more interested in pursuing arguments that are 'aimed at finding the truth' (p. 273). After five years of 'intensive study of philosophy', our students must return to 'the Cave', and take up a suitable military or administrative post (p. 273). At 50, those who have passed all the 'practical and intellectual tests' with greatest distinction should undergo their 'final trial': to 'lift their mind's eye to look at the source of all light, and see the good itself' (p. 273). They can then use this as 'a pattern' on which to base their own lives and that of society (p. 273). They will devote most of the rest of their lives to philosophy but, for society's sake will, in their turn, take up 'the weary business of politics' as Rulers (p. 273). And they will also have the task of training up successors.

Glaucon: This is a 'fine picture' of our Rulers (p. 274).

Socrates: And some of these will be women. But all this can only happen if 'true philosophers', whose main concern is 'doing right' and ensuring justice, have 'political power' (p. 274).

Glaucon: How would they get this process started?

Socrates: By removing children over ten from their parents, and their 'present way of life', and raising them 'on their own methods and rules' (p. 274). This will be the quickest way of establishing our new 'society and constitution' (p. 274).

Part IX   Imperfect Societies (pp. 275–334)

1   Recapitulation (pp. 276–8)

Socrates: Well, we have agreed that, 'in the perfect state', women and children should be 'held in common'; men and women should have the same education; the 'best at philosophy and war' should govern; and that the Guardians, who rule 'over the community', should not own private property, but 'devote themselves' to the care of the state (p. 276).

Glaucon: You said there are four wrong kinds of society. What are they?

Socrates: The '**Spartan** type', **oligarchy**, **democracy** and **tyranny**; and, to correspond to these and our 'ideal' type, there are 'five types of individual character' (p. 277). We need to examine these, to 'contrast the worst type of man with the best, and complete our enquiry into the relative happiness and unhappiness which pure justice and pure injustice bring' (pp. 277–8). Let us start with the first, 'ambitious' type of society, which we shall call '"**timarchy**" or "timocracy"' (p. 278).

2   Timarchy (pp. 278–82)

Socrates: Our 'ideal state' can become a timocracy, if there is dissension among 'the Auxiliaries and Rulers'; and this could happen if the Rulers get the 'times for breeding' wrong (pp. 278–9). Inopportune mating could result in children who are 'neither gifted nor lucky' (p. 280). When they take charge, they will neglect the education system, and will fail to 'distinguish the metals' of which the citizens are composed, resulting in the production of 'inconsistent and uneven material' (p. 280). When 'internal strife' starts, some Guardians will start to pursue 'private profit', while others try to maintain 'the traditional order of things' (p. 280). They will then reach a compromise, under which they will carve up the state's property among themselves, turning the other citizens, whom they formerly protected, into '**serfs and menials**' (p. 280). The resulting state will be halfway between 'the ideal and oligarchy' (p. 280). It will retain 'respect for authority', and emphasize 'physical and military training', while its 'soldier-class' will not become involved in business or agriculture, but it will resist appointment of the most intelligent to administrative posts, preferring 'hearty types, who prefer war to peace' (pp. 280–1).

Glaucon: I see.

Socrates: As their education has not included 'the true principles of a rational philosophic education', the Guardians will love money, which they will hoard in their 'private houses', and lavish on their wives (p. 281).

Glaucon: It sounds as if this society will be 'a mixture of good and evil' (p. 281).

Socrates: Yes, but it will be dominated by 'ambition and the competitive spirit' (p. 281).

3 The Timarchic Character (pp. 282–4)

Socrates: And there will be a type of individual corresponding to this society.

Adeimantus: I suppose he will be very 'competitive' (p. 282).

Socrates: He will be 'self-willed' and, as he will not be particularly 'well educated', he will treat his slaves harshly, because he will lack 'a proper sense of his superiority to them' (p. 282). He will be obedient to 'the authorities', ambitious for office (for which he will believe his 'military achievements' equip him), and he will enjoy 'exercise and hunting' (p. 282). As he gets older, he will love money more and more.

4 Oligarchy (pp. 284–7)

Socrates: Timocracy is destroyed by the 'accumulation of wealth in private hands' (p. 284). The 'ruling class' becomes 'extravagant' and greedy and, the more they value money, 'the less they value goodness' (pp. 284–5). We have a 'transition' from 'the ambitious, competitive type of man to the money-loving businessman' (p. 285). The rich are honoured, while the 'poor are despised' (p. 285). Legislation is introduced, which requires a 'certain minimum amount of property' for holding public office, and so 'an oligarchy is set up' (p. 285).

Adeimantus: What are 'its characteristic faults' (p. 285)?

Socrates: If we 'chose ships' captains on grounds of wealth', and excluded the poor, even though they were better sailors, we would get some bad navigation (p. 285). That is one weakness. Another is that society is split 'into two factions, the rich and the poor' (p. 286). Such a society is also unable 'to wage war', because 'the oligarchs' do not dare to arm the people, in case of rebellion (p. 286). People will be involved 'in many different occupations', which we have already condemned (p. 286). It will also be possible for an individual to sell all he owns, and 'live on as a member of society without any real function' (p. 286). And so a class of what we might call **'drones'** appears: mere consumers of goods (p. 286). The 'stingless' ones often turn into beggars, while the 'stinging type' become criminals (p. 287). This is what we end up with when 'power is linked with property' (p. 287).

5 The Oligarchic Character (pp. 287–90)

Socrates: The oligarchic type of man develops from the fact that this society reserves its admiration for 'the acquisition of wealth' (p. 288). The oligarchic man attaches 'overriding importance' to money (p. 288). He is 'economical and hard working' but, at the same time, 'always on the make' (p. 288). Although he will have a 'high reputation for honesty' in business matters, this is not due to '**moral conviction**', but to fear that a bad reputation would harm his standing in society (p. 289). Given a chance to cheat and get away with it, he will do so. He has a veneer of respectability, but lacks the 'real goodness of an integrated and balanced character' (p. 289).

6 Democracy (pp. 290–4)

Socrates: Absence of restraint in pursuit of wealth brings oligarchy to an end. The fact is 'love of money' and self-discipline are incompatible (p. 291). The rulers refuse to 'curtail by law the extravagance of the young', because they get rich from lending them money (p. 290). Some of the rulers spend their money recklessly, and end up in debt themselves. They become embittered against those they think have 'deprived them of their property', and 'long for revolution' (p. 291). The remaining oligarchs and their dependants become enfeebled by a life of 'luxury and idleness', and 'lose their ability to resist pain or pleasure' (p. 291). The society over which they preside becomes unhealthy and faction-ridden. Democracy comes into being when the poor overthrow the rulers, and give everybody '**equal civil rights** and opportunities of office' (p. 292).
Adeimantus: That is how it happens.
Socrates: Democracy seems 'the most attractive of all societies' (p. 293). It has 'liberty and freedom of speech'; the 'diversity of its characters' is appealing; it can contain 'every possible type' of constitution; and nobody is forced either to exercise, or submit to, authority (p. 293). It is a 'wonderfully pleasant way' of governing 'in the short run' (p. 293).
Adeimantus: 'In the short run, perhaps' (p. 293).

Socrates: And, of course, while we said that nobody would become a 'good man', unless 'trained in good habits' from the start, democracy disregards this approach, and cares nothing about 'the habits and background of its politicians' (p. 294). It is an '**anarchic form of society**', treating people as equal, even if they are not (p. 294).

7 The Democratic Character (pp. 294–8)

Socrates: We have '**necessary**' **desires**, as for food, which is essential for life and health, and 'unnecessary' ones, as for a 'luxurious diet', which may be 'physically harmful and psychologically damaging' (pp. 294–5). Now, our 'drone type', unlike the 'thrifty oligarchic type', will have many of the second kind of desires (p. 295). In our oligarchic society, young men, brought up in an 'economical way' by an oligarchic parent, may get a 'taste of the drones' honey', so that their 'internal oligarchy starts turning into a democracy' (p. 296). And, because of the failings of the education system, which means they lack 'sound knowledge' and 'true principles', unnecessary desires come to rule their lives (p. 296). Thus, they live 'from day to day, indulging the pleasure of the moment' (p. 298).

Adeimantus: A good description of those who believe in 'liberty and equality' (p. 298).

Socrates: Yes, this is the 'democratic man', who matches 'the variety of the democratic society'; and his life is one 'many men and women would envy' (p. 298).

8 Tyranny (pp. 298–308)

Socrates: In the same way that oligarchy was destroyed by 'excessive' pursuit of wealth, the objective for which it was established, democracy is destroyed by excessive pursuit of liberty, the objective for which it was established (p. 299). In its 'thirst for liberty', democracy falls into the hands of 'bad leaders', who flatter the public and fail to restrain them (p. 299). The citizens become 'so sensitive that the least vestige of restraint is resented as intolerable', and they 'disregard all laws written or unwritten' (p. 300). Now, this is 'the root from which tyranny springs' (p. 300).

Adeimantus: How so?

Socrates: We have already mentioned the 'class of thriftless idlers whom I compared to drones' (p. 301). Although, in an oligarchy, this group is excluded from power, in a democracy, 'practically all the leaders are drawn from it' (p. 302). As for the rest of society, there are those who seize the opportunity to make money, and become rich, and the 'mass of the people', who do not generally engage in politics, but who 'once assembled are supreme' (p. 302). The political leaders 'rob the rich', keep as much as they can for themselves, and throw the remainder to the masses, to keep them happy (p. 302). In the end, the rich, fed up with being plundered, speak out against the rulers, who accuse them of being '**reactionaries** and oligarchs' (p. 302). '**Impeachments** and trials' follow and, out of the confusion, a 'single **popular leader**' often emerges, whom the people entrust with the task of restoring order (p. 303).

Adeimantus: How does he turn into a tyrant?

Socrates: He becomes intoxicated with power, and starts a '**class war** against the owners of property' (p. 303). Then, protected by the 'personal bodyguard' he has insisted on having, he 'overthrows all opposition and grasps the reins of state, and stands, no longer champion, but the complete tyrant' (p. 304).

Adeimantus: 'That's the inevitable conclusion' (p. 304).

Socrates: So, now he must maintain his position. One way is by provoking wars, because a people at war will 'continue to need a leader', and it is an excuse for imposing heavy taxes (p. 304). He will root out actual or potential opponents, including any among those 'who helped him to power' (p. 305). He will employ a 'private army' of freed slaves and foreign mercenaries, and force the people to 'maintain him and his crew' (p. 307). The people saw him as their champion, who would 'free them from the power of the wealthy and so-called upper classes' (p. 307). Instead, they find that they have 'exchanged their excessive and untimely freedom for the harshest and bitterest of servitudes' (p. 308).

9 The Tyrannical Character (pp. 308–14)

Socrates: The 'individual of tyrannical character' is like one subject to a 'master passion' that 'runs wild and takes madness into its service'; either by 'birth or habit or both', it unites 'the characteristics of drunkenness, lust, and madness' (pp. 310–11).
Adeimantus: How does this type of man live?
Socrates: In his own life, he is addicted to an 'extravagant' lifestyle (p. 311). He spends what he has, then borrows and, when that runs out, seizes his parents' property. After that, he will turn to burglary and robbery; he will undertake 'any venture' which will profit him and his 'gang' (p. 312). And, if a state contains enough people of this type, 'the folly of the people helps them to produce a tyrant, and they pick the man who is at heart the completest and most absolute tyrant' (p. 313).
Adeimantus: He will be the 'best fitted for tyranny' (p. 313).
Socrates: If the people disobey him, he will 'punish his country' (p. 313). Tyrannical characters are the 'worst type' and 'perfect specimens of injustice' (p. 313).

10   *The Types of Character and Their Degrees of Happiness (pp. 314–30)*

(a) They rank in happiness in the order they were discussed (pp. 314–19)

Socrates: Clearly, 'the wickedest man will also prove to be the unhappiest', and the longer a tyrant reigns, the more unhappy he will be (p. 314). As the tyrannical man corresponds to the tyrannical state, and so on, 'in excellence and happiness the relations between the different types of individual will correspond to the relations between the different types of state' (p. 314). So, what is the 'relative excellence' of the tyrannical state and that ruled by 'philosopher kings' (p. 315)?

Glaucon: They are 'opposite extremes': the tyrannical state is the most unhappy, while none is 'happier than our philosopher kingship' (p. 315).

Socrates: Let us consider the 'characteristics' of the states and individuals (p. 315). Is the tyrannical state one of 'freedom or slavery' (p. 316)?

Glaucon: Complete slavery.

Socrates: The position of the tyrannical individual is 'analogous to the state' (p. 316). His 'best elements' will be in the thrall of 'the lowest and most lunatic impulses', which means that his mind is unable to do what it wants, while, like the tyrannical state, he will be 'haunted by fear' (p. 316).

Glaucon: So, he is 'the unhappiest of all men' (p. 317).

Socrates: He will be even unhappier if, instead of living as an ordinary citizen, he attains 'supreme power' (p. 317). Think of it this way. In normal circumstances, a 'private slave-owner', with many slaves, does not live in fear of them, because he has the support of his fellow citizens (p. 317). But, what if he were removed, with all his slaves, to 'some desert place' (p. 317)? Then, he would have reason to be afraid, and would need to 'curry favour' with some of his slaves, to protect himself against the rest (p. 317). And his situation would be even worse, if his neighbours were opposed to slavery. This is the tyrant's situation. He can never feel safe; his 'condition is utterly wretched' (p. 318).

Glaucon: It is undeniable.

Socrates: Thus, the happiest man is the philosopher king, who is 'sovereign over himself', and is the 'justest and the best' (p. 319). The tyrant, the 'unjustest and worst', is 'supremely wretched' (p. 319).

(b) The life of the just man and the philosopher is pleasanter than any other (pp. 319–23)

Socrates: We divided the mind into 'three elements', which give people 'understanding', 'spirit' and 'desire'; and this makes possible a further proof (pp. 319–20). Each element has its own 'particular pleasures' and 'governing principles' (p. 320). The third is motivated by 'profit or gain'; the second by 'ambition and love of honour'; and the first by 'discovery of the truth' (p. 320). We divide people into 'three basic types', according to whether they are motivated by 'knowledge, success or gain' (p. 320).

Glaucon: Surely.

Socrates: If each type was asked which of the lives the three types led was 'the pleasantest', he would choose his own (p. 321). And, if we compare them 'simply on the grounds of the amount of pleasure they give', without considering how 'admirable or how good or bad they are', it is hard to know the truth (p. 321). So, we need to ask which of them has 'the greatest experience of all three types of pleasure' (p. 321).

Glaucon: Well, the philosopher will know about gain, but the 'gain-lover' may not have experienced 'the pleasure of knowing the truth' (p. 321). Similarly, all three types have honour, if they achieve their objects, but 'only the philosopher can taste the pleasure of knowing the truth' (p. 322).

Socrates: So, the philosopher is best placed to judge, as he is the one in whom 'intelligence is joined with experience' and he has the 'necessary tools' (p. 322). Judgement is 'reached through reason', and 'rational argument' is his particular strength (p. 322). Thus, the pleasantest pleasure is that which belongs to the element 'which brings us knowledge', and the philosopher is right to prefer his own way of life (pp. 322–3). Which would he put second?

Glaucon: The soldier's.

Socrates: Making the 'pleasures of gain' last (p. 323).

(c) The philosopher's pleasures are the most real (pp. 323–9)

Socrates: Pleasure is the 'opposite of pain', and there is a state between the two, in which we feel neither (p. 323). And sometimes, when people are ill, they find 'relief from pain' to be the greatest pleasure, while those who are enjoying themselves find the cessation of pleasure painful (p. 324). So, rest, the 'intermediate state' between pleasure and pain, can be either pleasant or painful (p. 324)?

Glaucon: Yes.

Socrates: But we cannot say that 'absence of pain is pleasure', or vice-versa (p. 324). Rather, the 'state of rest' seems pleasant when contrasted with pain (or painful when contrasted with pleasure), but not when 'judged by the standard of true pleasure' (p. 324). So, 'pure pleasure' is not cessation of pain, nor 'pure pain' the ending of pleasure (p. 325). Of course, many people, not having experience of the truth, do not understand this, and think that the 'transition from pain to the neutral state brings satisfaction and pleasure' (p. 326). In the same way, they might think grey was white, if they had no experience of the latter.

Glaucon: Certainly.

Socrates: Now, which is 'more truly real': that which 'belongs to the realm of the unchanging and eternal truth', or that 'which belongs to the realm of change and mortality' (p. 326)?

Glaucon: The first.

Socrates: So, what 'supplies the needs of the body' is 'less true and less real' than that which 'supplies the needs of the mind' (p. 327). And the same is true of the body, 'compared with the mind' (p. 327). However, those who lack 'experience of wisdom and goodness' do not know this, just as they do not know the difference between what appears to be pleasure, in contrast to pain, and true pleasure (p. 327). And are not the pleasures of those who are ruled by their desires, and who 'stuff themselves and **copulate**', and 'kill each other' in their eagerness for more, 'inevitably mixed with pain, and so an empty sham and mere **phantoms of true pleasure**' (p. 327)?

Glaucon: You are describing the 'life of the common man' (p. 327).

Socrates: And, if a man pursues 'honour or success' without 'sense or reason', does not this lead to 'envy and violence' (p. 328).

Glaucon: Inevitably.

Socrates: Our pursuit of gain and ambition must be guided by 'knowledge and reason' (p. 328). That way, we shall seek only the pleasures indicated by wisdom, which will be 'the truest' (p. 328). If our minds are ruled by the 'philosophic element', all its elements will be just, and each will fulfil 'its own function' (p. 328). However, if one of the other elements predominates, the other elements will 'pursue a false pleasure' (p. 328).

Glaucon: True.

Socrates: And this is most likely to occur if the element 'furthest removed from philosophy and reason' is in control, because that will be the most remote from 'law and order': which, of course, is the case with 'tyrannical desires' (p. 328). So, the tyrant is furthest away from true pleasure, and leads the 'most unpleasant' life, while the 'philosopher king', who is closest to it, has the 'most pleasant' (pp. 328–9).

(d) The tyrant is 729 times more unhappy than the philosopher king (pp. 329–30)

Socrates: As the tyrant surrounds himself with **'spurious types' of pleasure**, his 'degree of inferiority' is hard to describe (p. 329). However, if we calculate it mathematically, on the basis of the 'three types of pleasure', the philosopher 'lives seven hundred and twenty-nine times more pleasantly than the tyrant' (pp. 329–30).

Glaucon: That highlights the gulf between the 'just and unjust man in terms of pleasure and pain' (p. 330).

Socrates: And think how infinitely 'superior' the just man is 'in terms of grace and beauty of life and of excellence' (p. 330).

11 Conclusion (pp. 330–4)

Socrates: What, then, of the claim that wrongdoing pays, provided that one can combine 'complete injustice with a reputation for justice' (p. 330)? Let us think of the 'human personality' as three creatures: a **many-headed beast**, a lion and a man, merged into one, with the 'external appearance' of the man (pp. 330–1). Saying that doing wrong is to an individual's advantage, is to say that free rein should be given to the many-headed beast, and encouragement to the lion, while the man within him should be starved until 'the other two can do what they like with him' (p. 331).

Glaucon: That would be practising 'justice and wrongdoing' (p. 331).

Socrates: But saying the individual profits by being just is saying we should 'strengthen the man within us', so that he can control the many-headed beast, and make the lion 'an ally' (p. 331). To do wrong is to enslave 'the divinest part of oneself to the most godless and abominable' (p. 332). We cannot argue that it is to an individual's advantage to be 'unjust or self-indulgent or do anything base'; doing so may give him 'money and power', but he will be 'a worse man' (p. 333). And, if he gets away with it, he will grow even worse. Being detected may enable him to master the beast within him, so that he can develop a character which combines 'self-control and justice and understanding' (p. 333). This is what the intelligent man will aim at: he will value only studies 'that form his mind and character accordingly' (p. 334).

Glaucon: Then he will not enter politics.

Socrates: He will in 'the society where he really belongs' (p. 334).

Glaucon: The one we have described, but it may well never 'exist on earth' (p. 334).

Socrates: Perhaps it is 'a pattern in heaven', which those wishing to do so can see and lay down in their own hearts (p. 334).

Part X   Theory of Art (pp. 335–53)

1   *Art and Illusion (pp. 335–45)*

Socrates: As you know, there is 'a single form for each set of particular things' so, although there are many beds, there is only one form of a bed (p. 336). Somebody making a bed observes 'the appropriate form', but could not 'make the form itself' (pp. 336–7).

Glaucon: No.

Socrates: What if a craftsman existed, who could not only make 'all artificial objects', but everything in the world as well (p. 337)? You could do so yourself.

Glaucon: How?

Socrates: By using a mirror.

Glaucon: But they would be reflections, not 'real things' (p. 337).

Socrates: Quite right. Let us return to the bed. There are 'three sorts': that 'in nature', which is 'the form of bed'; that made by the carpenter, which is not 'ultimately real' and is a 'shadowy thing compared to reality'; and the painter's (pp. 337–8). God created the 'only one real bed-in-itself in nature' (p. 338). The carpenter manufactures a particular bed. What about the artist?

Glaucon: He 'represents what the other two make' (p. 339).

Socrates: Which is 'at third remove from reality', just as the tragic poet's representation is 'at third remove from the throne of truth' (p. 339). Further, this representation is not of objects as they actually are, but of their 'superficial appearance' (p. 339). When somebody tells us that **tragedians**, such as Homer, 'know all about human excellence and defect and about religion', we must keep it in mind that their representations are of 'appearances and not realities' (p. 340). Further, if a man knew about the things he represented, would he not address them, rather than just represent them?

Glaucon: His service would be greater if he did.

Socrates: Homer writes about 'military strategy' and 'political administration', but did he ever reform a state's constitution, or command a successful army (p. 341)?

Glaucon: No.

Socrates: Nor was he an inventor or educator. In fact, Homer and all the other poets just 'produce a superficial likeness of any subject they treat, including human excellence', but the 'natural magic of poetry' gives the impression they have something to say (p. 342). Think of it like this. The user of something knows the most about how it functions; its maker will depend on his knowledge, and so have 'a **correct** *belief*' about it (pp. 343–4). However, poets and artists have neither knowledge nor correct belief, and so are 'beautifully ill-informed' about the things they represent (p. 344). Thus, representing things has 'no serious value', and this is particularly so of 'tragic poetry' (p. 344).

2 *The Appeal of Art and Poetry (pp. 345–9)*

Socrates: When our reason, on the basis of calculation and measurement, tells us that one thing is greater than another, 'it may be contradicted by appearances' (p. 346). As the part that calculates and measures must be our 'best part', that which contradicts must be 'an inferior one' (p. 346). As 'representative artists' deal with appearances, their work is distant from reason and truth (p. 346). Let us think specifically about '**dramatic poetry**', and 'the part of the mind' to which it appeals (p. 346).

Glaucon: 'That's what we should do' (p. 346).

Socrates: We feel grief if we lose somebody close to us, but 'reason and principle demand restraint' (p. 347). An internal element of 'deliberation' counsels us to 'bear misfortune patiently', while our irrational element urges us to indulge our feelings (p. 348). The 'dramatic poet' directs his work towards the latter element, because it is easier to portray an 'unstable and **refractory**' character than the 'reasonable element' in human beings (p. 348). Thus, he reinforces the 'lower elements' of the human personality at the expense of reason, which is like letting the 'worst elements' in society govern the state (pp. 348–9).

3 The Effects of Poetry and Drama (pp. 349–53)

Socrates: Poetry can 'corrupt even the best characters' (p. 349). Think how we all enjoy the 'sufferings of a hero' and the 'sounds and signs of tragic grief', praising the poet who portrays them 'most powerfully' (p. 349). Yet, in life, we admire 'just the opposite' (p. 349). The poet encourages us to indulge those '**instinctive desires**' that we would normally restrain (p. 350). We feel doing so is all right, because the play concerns 'someone else's sufferings' (p. 350). Again, we laugh at jokes on stage, which we 'would be ashamed' to make ourselves (p. 350). And it is the same with all the 'desires and feelings of pleasure and pain' portrayed in poetry (p. 350).

Glaucon: There is no denying it.

Socrates: The only role poetry 'should be allowed in a state' is honouring the gods and praising good men (p. 351). Those of us brought up 'to love poetry' will find it hard to renounce, but we must stand firm against 'falling under the spell of childish and vulgar passion' (p. 352). Poetry has no 'claim to truth', and damages the composition of our 'inner selves' (p. 352). What confronts us here is 'the choice between becoming a good man or a bad' (p. 352).

Part XI The Immortality of the Soul and the Rewards of Goodness (pp. 354–68)

1 The Soul Immortal (pp. 354–8)

Socrates: But we have not touched on the 'chief rewards' of goodness (p. 354). You know that our **soul** is '**immortal** and never perishes' (p. 354).

Glaucon: 'Good Lord, no! Are you prepared to maintain that it is' (p. 354)?

Socrates: It is not 'difficult' (p. 354). We use 'the terms good and evil': evil 'destroys', and good 'preserves and benefits' (pp. 354–5). Each thing has 'its own **particular good**', but also its evil (p. 355). The body, for example, is subject to illness; and it is a thing's **particular evil** that destroys it. However, if there is something that cannot be destroyed by its particular evil, we shall know that it is 'indestructible' (p. 355). So, what 'makes the soul evil' (p. 355)?

Glaucon: Such things as 'injustice, indiscipline, cowardice and ignorance' (p. 355).

Socrates: Now the question is: Does a 'flaw in the soul', such as injustice, lead to its 'annihilation', in the same way that disease destroys the body (p. 355)?

Glaucon: No.

Socrates: And it would be 'quite illogical' to think that one thing's particular evil could destroy another thing (p. 356). Thus, a 'bodily flaw' cannot destroy the soul (p. 356). Injury and disease do not affect the soul: unless we believe that they make the soul 'more unjust or wicked than it was' (p. 356).

Glaucon: There is no evidence that 'death makes the soul more wicked' (p. 356).

Socrates: Then, if no evil, 'either its own or another's', can destroy the soul, it 'must be immortal' (p. 357). And, this being the case, **the same souls must always have existed**: their number cannot increase or decrease. Further, we must not think of the soul as **composed of parts**; if it were, it would not be immortal (p. 357).

Glaucon: It could not.

Socrates: We have proved the soul's immortality. However, to see what it is really like, we need to see it, not as it is now, 'deformed by its association with the body and other evils, but in the pure state which reason reveals to us' (pp. 357–8). Think of the soul's 'kinship with the divine and immortal', and imagine what it could become, if it pursued its 'love of wisdom' wholeheartedly (p. 358).

2   *The Rewards of Goodness in this Life (pp. 358–60)*

Socrates: Justice is 'the best thing for our true self', and so we should be just (pp. 358–9). I shall now outline the present and future rewards that 'men and gods' give to the just man (p. 359). However, Glaucon, I must ask you to 'give up the concession' I made earlier: that the just man should have a reputation for wickedness and vice-versa (p. 359). This was done to enable us to 'judge between justice and injustice in themselves, without their consequences' (p. 359). Now I want to 'restore Justice her good name' (p. 359). After all, you would accept that the gods know who is just and unjust?
Glaucon: Yes.
Socrates: That being so, they will love the just man, who may expect all 'the blessings' of heaven, apart from **punishments for 'offences committed in a former life'** (p. 359). The unjust man can expect the opposite. And, if a just man suffers in this life, it must be for 'his ultimate good in this life or the next', as the gods would not ignore him (p. 360). Furthermore, in this life, even if the unjust man fares well in the short term, is it not the just man who, in the longer term, 'gets both the rewards and the good name among his fellows' (p. 360)?
Glaucon: Yes.
Socrates: The just man, as he gets older, will hold 'positions of authority in the state', but the unjust man's 'old age will be miserable' (p. 360).

3 The Myth of Er (pp. 361–8)

(a) The just man's rewards in the life after death (pp. 361–3)

Socrates: These are the just man's rewards in this life, 'over and above those which justice herself brings him' (p. 361). But they are nothing in comparison to what awaits 'the just man and unjust man after death' (p. 361).

Glaucon: I would like to hear about them.

Socrates: I will tell you the story of 'Er, son of Armenius' (p. 361). Killed in battle, he was taken home for burial. However, he came back to life on the funeral pyre, and described his experiences in 'the other world' (p. 361). After his soul left his body, it travelled to a place where there were 'two gaping chasms' in both the earth and the sky (p. 361). Judges sat between them who, after examining the **evidence for judgement** each soul carried, ordered the just to proceed up to the sky, while the unjust were sent down into the earth. However, they told Er to watch and listen, as he was to be 'a messenger to men about the other world' (p. 361). As well as seeing souls, after they had been judged, entering the heavenly or earthly chasms, he saw souls emerging from them, and then setting up camp in the fields. Er listened to the souls discussing their experiences of either underground sufferings, which had 'lasted a thousand years', or 'the delights of heaven' (p. 362). Those who had done wrong had to 'pay tenfold in suffering for each offence', while the good were 'rewarded in the same proportion' (p. 362). And the punishments of those who had committed murder, or dishonoured the gods or their parents, were even greater. When the mouth of the chasm refused to receive certain murderous tyrants, 'fierce and fiery-looking men' seized and flayed them, and 'impaled them on thorns by the roadside' (pp. 362–3).

(b) The structure of the universe (pp. 363–8)

Socrates: The souls left the camp after seven days, and journeyed to a place where they saw a 'shaft of light stretching from above straight through earth and heaven, like a pillar' (p. 363). This was the '**bond of heaven**', which holds together its circumference (p. 363). From its ends hangs the '**spindle of Necessity**', which makes 'all the **orbits** to revolve' (p. 363). The spindle's '**whorl**' comprises a large, 'hollowed out' whorl, into which exactly fits a smaller one, and into that another, and so on 'to a total of eight' (pp. 363–4). The whorls form 'the continuous surface of a single whorl round the shaft', and their rims are of different colours (p. 364). The whole spindle 'revolved with a single motion' but, within it, 'the seven inner circles' revolved in the opposite direction, the whole spindle turning 'in the **lap of Necessity**' (p. 364). A siren, emitting 'a note of constant pitch', stands on the top of each circle, and round it sit 'the **three Fates, daughters of Necessity**': **Lachesis** (things past); **Clotho** (things present); and **Atropos** (things to come) (p. 364). The souls went first before Lachesis, and 'an Interpreter', taking from her lap 'a number of lots and **patterns of life**', declared: 'Souls of a day, here you must begin another round of mortal life whose end is death' (pp. 364–5). He warned that they were choosing for themselves, and they were responsible for the consequences of their choice, not God. Then he threw down the lots, which would decide the order in which the souls would make their choice, and placed before them numerous patterns of life from which they could choose. They included tyrannies, 'strength and athletic prowess' and eminent birth; and there were as many choices for women as for men (p. 365). It was not possible to choose 'quality of character': each soul had to take on a character 'appropriate to its choice', and this would contain a mixture of such elements as wealth or poverty, and health or disease (p. 365).

And this, Glaucon, is why it is so important to discover who or what will enable us 'to tell a good life from a bad one' (p. 365). We need to know what impact such factors as wealth, poverty and different types of character have on our lives, so that we can decide, given 'how the soul is constituted', which will help us to lead the more just and better life (pp. 365–6). We must hang on to this knowledge when we 'enter the other world', so that we avoid the temptations of wealth and power; and, in this life and the next, we must 'choose the middle course', which leads to 'the highest human happiness' (p. 366).

Er said that the souls began to choose, and the first, ignoring the interpreter's warning, chose 'the greatest tyranny he could find', without taking into account the fact that it would involve terrible crimes and suffering (p. 366). Some of those from heaven chose precipitately, because they lacked 'the discipline of suffering', while those from the earth tended to choose more carefully, because of the suffering they had undergone (p. 366). The choices made were interesting. **Odysseus**, for example, whose ambitions had caused him so much suffering, chose 'the uneventful life of an ordinary man' (p. 367). Next, Lachesis appointed a '**Guardian Spirit**' to guide each soul in life (p. 367). He led the soul to Clotho, who confirmed the choice, and after that, to Atropos, who made the '**threads of its destiny irreversible**' (p. 367). Finally, each soul went before 'the **throne of Necessity**', and then, after waiting until all the souls had done so, moved on to 'the plain of **Lethe**' (pp. 367–8). That evening they camped 'by the **Forgetful River**', from which they had to drink; and as each did so, 'he forgot everything' (p. 368). At midnight, there was 'an earthquake and thunder', and all the souls were carried away 'to their birth' (p. 368).

We must remember this story, Glaucon, so that when

we cross the 'river of Lethe', 'we shall not defile our souls' (p. 368). We must always be mindful of the fact that our soul is immortal, and we must 'pursue justice with wisdom' (p. 368). By doing so, we shall be 'at peace with the gods and with ourselves'; and 'all will be well with us' in this life and the next (p. 368).

Overview

The following section is a chapter-by-chapter overview of the II chapters in Plato's *The Republic*, designed for quick reference to the detailed summary above.

Readers may also find this section helpful for revision.

The characters are: Socrates, Glaucon, Adeimantus, Polemarchus, Cephalus, Thrasymachus, Lysias, Euthydemus, Charmantides and Cleitophon.

Part I   Introduction (pp. 3–52)

1   Prelude (pp. 3–8)

Socrates explains how he accompanied Glaucon to the Piraeus for a religious festival, where they met Polemarchus and Adeimantus. At the former's house, they discuss right and wrong and Cephalus' view that it consists of truthfulness and always returning borrowed items.

2   The Conventional View of Justice Developed (pp. 8–15)

Polemarchus supports his father's view. Doing right is giving everyone his due, and justice consists of helping friends (good and honest people) and injuring enemies (the opposite). Socrates refers to difficulties of identifying the good and honest people, arguing that, as justice concerns human excellence, and bad men will become worse, if harmed, justice cannot be giving people their due, if this involves harming enemies.

3 Thrasymachus and the Rejection of Conventional Morality (pp. 15–40)

(a) First Statement and Criticisms (pp. 15–24)

Thrasymachus argues that what is right is whatever is in the interests of government, the strongest power in the state. Socrates points out that governments may misjudge their own interests, which would make it right for subjects to obey laws that are not in the strongest power's interests. He also argues that those with professional skills, such as doctors, exercise them for others' benefit, not their own. The same is true of those in government, whose concern is with their subjects' interests.

(b) Second Statement and Final Refutation (pp. 24–40)

Thrasymachus claims that shepherds look after their flocks to make a profit from them. In the same way, justice is someone else's good: the ruler's at the subject's expense. Unjust people always fare better, and are happier, than just ones, especially if, like tyrants, they do wrong on a grand scale. People condemn wrongdoing through fear of suffering, not doing, it. Socrates points out that Thrasymachus has shifted his ground, having previously accepted that the exercise of a professional skill, including governing, benefits the subject, not the practitioner. In a city of good men, there would be competition to avoid power, as they would not wish to be accused of pursuing self-interest.

(i) The just man is wise and good, and the unjust man is bad and ignorant (pp. 30–4)

Socrates shows that the unjust man is bad and ignorant because, unlike the just man, he competes with other unjust men, as well as with just men. The just man, on the other hand, competes only with unjust men; therefore, he is the one with knowledge, and who is wise and good.

(ii) Injustice is a source of disunity and weakness (pp. 34–7)

Socrates also shows that, to succeed, unjust people must behave justly. The citizens of an aggressor state, or a band of thieves, could not succeed in their objectives, if they wronged each other. Injustice leads to quarrels, ruling out cooperative effort.

(iii) The just man is happier than the unjust (pp. 37–40)

Socrates argues that something with a function has its own particular excellence. As justice is the particular excellence of the mind, the just man, with a just mind, will lead a good life, while the unjust man will lead a bad one. As the man with the good life is prosperous and happy, it is the just, not the unjust man, who is happy.

4 Adeimantus and Glaucon Restate the Case for Injustice (pp. 40–52)

(a) Justice and morality are merely a matter of convenience (pp. 40–6)

Glaucon is not convinced that right action is always better than wrong. He divides good things into three categories: those, like pleasure, wanted for their own sake; those, like wisdom, wanted for their own sake and their consequences; and those, like medical treatment, which, though painful, are chosen for their benefits. He asks Socrates where justice and right belong. Socrates puts them in the second category, which is the highest.

Glaucon than argues that most people put them in the third.

Reviving Thrasymachus' argument, he refers to the common opinion that it is good to inflict wrong, but bad to suffer it. We cannot always inflict wrong, or avoid suffering it, so agree to prevent both. Justice is the middle ground between what is most and least desirable. People would prefer to do wrong, but cannot, and so practise justice unwillingly. No one believes justice pays; even so-called just men pursue self-interest, if they can get away with it. Unjust men often prosper, while just men can lead miserable lives. Gods and men seem to offer a better life to the unjust than the just.

(b) People do right only for what they can get out of it
(pp. 46–52)

Adeimantus points out that justice is commended, not because it is valued in itself, but for the good reputation and heavenly rewards it brings. Unjust men are respected as long as they are rich and powerful, and maintain a veneer of respectability. The advocates of justice should show the ill effects of injustice, and the beneficial effects of justice, on the mind. He urges Socrates to do so.

Part II   Preliminaries (pp. 53–66)

1   First Principles of Social Organization (pp. 53–60)

Socrates stresses the difficulty of determining the nature of justice, and argues that, to start with, it may be easier to identify in society than the individual. He describes a primitive society, which comes into being because of individuals' lack of self-sufficiency and for the benefits of people being able to specialize in different tasks.

2 *Civilized Society (pp. 60–3)*

Responding to Glaucon's objection, Socrates concedes that he is not describing a civilized society which, as it would not be limited to necessities, would require a wider range of specialized occupations. As it would want to acquire territory from neighbouring states, it would need an army which, to be effective, must be a professional one.

3 *Qualities Required in the Guardians (pp. 63–6)*

Socrates maintains that a society requires a Guardian class, to defend and govern it. They must be philosophers because, as well as being, like watchdogs, savage to strangers, they must be gentle to their fellow citizens and love learning.

Part III   Education: The First Stage (pp. 67–111)

1 *Secondary or Literary Education (pp. 67–100)*

(a) Current Literature Unsuitable Theologically (pp. 67–76)

To prepare them for their role, the Guardians need a suitable educational programme of mental and physical training, the content of which must be carefully controlled. Socrates outlines it. To promote excellence of character, the fiction they read must not misrepresent the nature of gods and heroes. It must show the gods as perfect in beauty and goodness. Books and plays that do not do so must be banned.

(b) Current Literature Unsuitable Morally (pp. 76–85)

To foster military virtues, fiction must inculcate courage and diminish fear of death. It must contain inspiring tales of endurance by famous men, but not any that show unjust men as happy, or which suggest that wrongdoing pays.

(c) Formal Requirements of Literature (pp. 85–93)

As the future Guardians will have the job of running the state, if they read aloud from plays, they must only act the parts of courageous and pious men.

(d) Musical Requirements (pp. 93–6)

Musical works must portray brave men of moderation and common sense on military service and in appropriate peace-time occupations.

(e) Summary (pp. 96–100)

The aim of the educational programme is to cultivate good character. Artists must be capable of perceiving the real nature of what is beautiful, so that their works influence young people for good. The future Guardians will not be properly educated, unless they recognize such qualities as discipline, courage, generosity and greatness of mind.

2   Physical Education (pp. 100–11)

The future Guardians require basic physical training, to make them alert and capable of military service. They must avoid luxurious living and being fussy about their health. Society needs citizens with good physical and psychological constitutions. It should leave the unhealthy to die, and kill those with corrupt psychological constitutions. The aim of the Guardians' mental and physical training is to ensure that they have a proper balance between their reason and their energy and initiative.

Detailed Summary of Plato's The Republic

Part IV   Guardians and Auxiliaries (pp. 112–29)

1   *The Three Classes and Their Mutual Relations* (pp. 112–17)

Socrates explains that the elder, best and most intelligent Guardians, who will always do what is best for their community, must rule. Future Guardians must be carefully monitored, to ensure adherence to this principle. Auxiliary Guardians will be required, to assist the Rulers and serve in the army.

He recommends having a magnificent myth about society's origin, to reinforce members' acceptance of their particular role. All are brother members of the community, but God put gold in those capable of ruling; silver in the Auxiliaries; and bronze or iron in the rest. Usually, children will be like their parents, but not always. Guardians must check the metal of all children, promoting or demoting them, as necessary, to the class for which their abilities equip them.

2   *The Rulers' and Auxiliaries' Way of Life (pp. 117–21)*

Socrates warns that the Guardians' way of life must exclude the possibility of their preying on their fellow citizens. They must live together in barracks, and not own private property. He rejects as irrelevant Adeimantus' point that they will not be happy. The aim of his proposed system of government is not the Guardians' happiness, but the welfare of the whole community.

3 Final Provisions for Unity (pp. 121–9)

Socrates insists that the Guardians must prevent extremes of wealth and poverty among their fellow citizens, as they are socially disruptive. He dismisses Adeimantus' worry that the new state, lacking wealth, will be unable to fight off a powerful enemy. Its professional army will be able to defeat an army three times its size while, unlike its enemies, it will be united and free of conflict between rich and poor.

Part V Justice in State and Individual (pp. 130–56)

1 Justice in the State (pp. 131–9)

Socrates explains that such a society will be wise (due to the Guardians' knowledge); courageous (due to the way its soldier-class upholds its values); and self-disciplined (due to government by its best members, with the whole community's consent). It will be just, because the members of its three classes (businessmen, Auxiliaries and Guardians) do the job for which they are most suited. Thus, justice is doing one's own job and not attempting jobs for which one is unsuited.

2 The Elements in Mental Conflict (pp. 139–49)

Like society, the human personality consists of three elements: reason; the irrational appetite; and reason's ally, spirit or indignation (which a person feels when his desires impel him to actions of which reason disapproves).

3 *Justice in the Individual (pp. 149–54)*

Justice in the individual is the three elements minding their own business, with reason, supported by spirit, ruling, and thus controlling the irrational appetite, leading to a well-disciplined individual.

4 *Conclusion (pp. 154–6)*

Glaucon claims it is absurd to believe that a life, which does not include acting justly and honourably, is worth living. Socrates suggests they should examine the various types of political constitution, and the types of human character each fosters. There are five: theirs (which is good) and four bad ones.

Part VI Women and the Family (pp. 157–88)

1 *The Status of Women (pp. 157–67)*

Before they can do so, Adeimantus asks for more details of the Guardians' family life. This leads Socrates to argue that, as there are no relevant intellectual or physical differences between men and women, the latter should have the same intellectual and physical training as men, and become Guardians (Rulers and Auxiliaries).

2 *Marriage and the Family (pp. 167–82)*

The Guardians must not have their own households, or own private property. Women and children should be held in common, so that parents and children do not know each other. Through a system of lots, the Rulers must ensure that the most gifted and healthy Guardians breed often, so that talented children are produced, and that less gifted and healthy Guardians have few opportunities to do so. Children will be taken to a state nursery at birth, and weak or defective children disposed of. Female Guardians will be allowed to breed between the ages of 20 and 40, men from 25 to 55. Although Guardians can mate freely outside these age ranges, it will be a crime for them to produce children; births must be prevented, or the children disposed of. To prevent incest, men (and women) will regard all children born within ten months of their mating as sons and daughters; their children as grandchildren; and so on.

These arrangements will ensure that the state's rulers and subjects regard each other as fellow citizens, while uniting the Guardian class, who will regard themselves as members of one family. There will be none of the dissension that arises when rulers accumulate wealth for themselves, or promote their own family interests.

3   The Rules of War (pp. 182–8)

Both men and women will serve in the army. The brave (in their lifetimes and posthumously) will be honoured, and cowards and deserters will be expelled from the Guardian class. Greeks should not fight each other, or sell one another into slavery. Wars should be fought only against the barbarians, while wars within Greece should be regarded (and condemned) as civil strife.

Part VII   The Philosopher Ruler (pp. 189–248)

1   *The Ideal and the Actual (pp. 189–92)*

Socrates puts forward what he accepts is a controversial view: that the problems of existing states (and humanity) will not end until philosophers become kings, or current rulers become philosophers.

2   *Definition of the Philosopher (pp. 192–208)*

(a) The Philosopher and the Two Orders of Reality
(pp. 192–204)

Socrates explains why this is so. People may recognize individual just acts or beautiful objects, but cannot see the essential nature of justice or beauty, and so have only opinions about them. The philosopher sees the essential nature of justice or beauty, as well as the things that share them, and so has knowledge. Opinion is in an intermediate position between knowledge and ignorance, and many conventional views about beauty and other important issues occupy this intermediate position between what is not and what fully is.

(b) The Qualities of Character Required in the Philosopher
(pp. 204–8)

As philosophers can grasp the eternal and immutable, can see the forms that underlie each reality, and so have a clear standard of right and good, on which to base the rules they impose, they should rule the state.

3   The Prejudice Against Philosophy and the Corruption of the Philosophic Nature in Contemporary Society (pp. 208–19)

Socrates deals with Adeimantus' objection that philosophers often seem useless. Society is unwilling to listen to good philosophers; bogus philosophers give philosophy a bad name; and those with a potential for philosophy may become discouraged, corrupted by the flattery of the masses, distracted by pursuit of the good life, or so disgusted with contemporary society that they devote themselves to private study, rather than politics.

4   The Philosopher Ruler Is Not Impossible (pp. 219–25)

Socrates identifies a further problem: people begin to study philosophy at too early an age, when their minds are immature, and give it up too soon. The tragedy is that neither a perfect society, nor perfect individuals, can be created until true philosophers engage in politics. Society needs to understand that true philosophers are those whose minds are focused on the immutable realities, where all is order and reason, and there is no injustice. They will be able to develop a new and better social system, based on their study of the true nature of justice, beauty and self-discipline. Once philosophers are established as rulers, people will see the benefits, and obey them willingly.

5 *The Good as Ultimate Object of Knowledge (pp. 226–35)*

(a) *The Qualities of Character the Philosopher Must Have* (pp. 226–31)

Philosophers who govern states must love their country; have characters that combine the qualities of mental quickness and reliability; and, above all, be able to reach the highest form of knowledge – the form of the good. Those without this knowledge are ignorant of what is good and valuable, and may think (as many do) that pleasure is the good. In response to Glaucon's question as to what the good is, Socrates admits he is unable to say what it is in itself, but can describe something closely resembling it.

(b) *The Simile of the Sun* (pp. 231–5)

Particular good things are distinguished from the single form of the good, which is not visible, but an object of intelligence. Just as the sun is not sight or the eye, but we cannot see without it, the form of the good's relation to intelligence and intelligible objects, in the intelligible world, is like the sun's to sight and visible objects in the visible world. When the mind focuses on objects illuminated by truth and reality, it can know and understand them but, in the ordinary world of change and decay, it can only form opinions about them. The form of the good provides objects of knowledge with their intelligibility and reality, and individuals with their ability to know.

6 *The Analogy of the Divided Line (pp. 235–40)*

Socrates asks his listeners to keep in mind the two orders of things, the visible and the intelligible, with the sun and the form of the good supreme over them. They should think of a line, divided into two unequal parts, and divided again in the same ratio.

For the visible world, this gives one subsection (D) for images (shadows and reflections) and another (C) for their originals (animals and plants). The difference between the two sub-sections is that one is genuine, the other not, and the relation between them is that of the realm of opinion to that of knowledge. For the intelligible world, in one subsection (B), the mind (as in geometry) uses the originals of the visible order as images; bases its inquiries on assumptions; and moves from them to a conclusion, not a first principle. In the other (A), by the use of dialectic, it goes from assumptions to a first principle, without the use of images, proceeding solely through the forms themselves. Subsection (A) of the intelligible world, studied by dialectic, is much clearer than (B), studied by the sciences because, although the latter's subject-matter involves reason, not sense-perception, it regards assumptions as first principles, moving from them, rather than to a first principle. There are four states of mind, corresponding to the four sections of the line: intelligence, reason, belief and illusion.

7   The Simile of the Cave (pp. 240–8)

Human enlightenment or ignorance is like an underground cave, containing men, imprisoned from childhood, who cannot turn their heads. Behind and above them is a fire and, between it and them, a road (also above them), in front of which is a wall. People carry different objects along the road, which show above the wall, but the prisoners see only the shadows, projected on to the wall opposite them. Therefore, they would regard the shadows as real things. A released prisoner, who turned towards the fire, would be too dazzled to see the real objects properly; would still think that the shadows were reality; and would be unable to see anything in the upper world. But, in the end, able to look directly at the sun, he would realize it controls everything in the visible world, and would not want to return to his previous opinions.

If he revisited the cave, he would be blinded by the darkness, and his former companions would say his time in the upper world had ruined his sight. The cave is the visible world, and the light of the fire is the power of the sun. The ascent to the upper world is the mind's progress to the intelligible region, where the last thing to be seen is the form of the good, familiarity with which is essential for rational action.

Understandably, those who have seen it prefer to remain in the intelligible world, and find it difficult to discuss what is just with those who have never seen justice itself. However, those who are ignorant of truth cannot rule society well. The best minds must attain the vision of the good, but then return to government. Socrates dismisses Glaucon's observation that doing so will impoverish the philosophers' lives. The aim is the welfare of the whole of society. Philosophers must understand they have been specially trained to govern, for which knowledge of the truth about justice and the good equips them. Their distaste for power will make them better rulers.

Part VIII   The Education of the Philosopher
(pp. 249–74)

1   *Preliminary (pp. 249–54)*

Socrates describes the programme of advanced studies, which will enable the trainee philosophers to see the form of the good. Number is one of them.

2 The Five Mathematical Studies (pp. 254–63)

(a) Arithmetic (pp. 254–6)

Understanding the nature of numbers by pure thought will lead students' minds towards truth.

(b) Plane Geometry (pp. 256–8)

Geometry is valuable, because it requires students to contemplate reality rather than the realm of change.

(c) Solid Geometry (pp. 258–9)

This is a useful subject, in which there will be further progress with state encouragement.

(d) Astronomy (pp. 259–61)

This will not be mere observation of the stars, which may be the most perfect things in the realm of change, but are inferior to the true realities. The focus will be on solving the problems posed by astronomy.

(e) Harmonics (pp. 262–3)

This will not be about music as such; it will be approached in the same way as astronomy.

3 Dialectic (pp. 263–7)

Students will pursue these studies, until they understand their common ground and relationship. However, only dialectic, which depends on reason without aid from the senses, and which destroys all assumptions, will move their minds out of the shadows, and enable them to grasp, by pure thought, what the good is in itself. A dialectician penetrates to the essential nature of each thing, including the good. Those, who cannot define the form of the good, do not know what the good is in itself; cannot identify particular good things; and so have opinion, not knowledge.

4   Selection and Curriculum (pp. 267–74)

Students must have a natural aptitude for these studies, be eager to learn, brave and have moral integrity. They will start the course as children, and there will be further selection, at 20, of those who are able to see how the different subjects are related to each other. Further selection, at 30, will be of those with the ability to follow truth into the realm of pure reality, without the aid of the senses. Socrates warns of the dangers of dialectic. People learn conventional opinions about right and wrong from their parents, but when they hear these views successfully challenged in debate, may conclude that there is no difference between right and wrong. This is a consequence of their starting philosophy too young. They become addicted to argument, and reject all their beliefs, which discredits philosophy. It is important that students of philosophy are self-disciplined, and committed to pursuit of the truth.

After five years of intensive philosophical study, the students must give it up for a time, and take up suitable military or administrative posts. At 50, the most able will undergo their final test – that of seeing the good itself. Having done so, they can use it as a pattern, on which to base their own lives and society's. They will devote most of the rest of their lives to philosophy but will, in turn, take up the task of politics as Rulers (there will be both men and women), and also train their successors.

Socrates emphasizes that this will not happen, unless true philosophers, concerned with doing right and ensuring justice, have political power. To start the process, children should be removed from their parents, and educated in the way described.

Part IX   Imperfect Societies (pp. 275–334)

1   *Recapitulation (pp. 276–8)*

Glaucon asks for more information about the four bad kinds of society Socrates had mentioned. They are timarchy, oligarchy, democracy and tyranny, each of which produces a certain type of human character.

2   *Timarchy (pp. 278–82)*

The ideal state can become a timarchy if, as a result of the Rulers mismanaging the breeding and educational programmes, unsuitable children are trained as Guardians. Quarrels may break out among Auxiliaries and Rulers, as some pursue private profit, while others try to uphold the traditional order of things. They may then divide up the state's property among themselves, turning the other citizens into serfs. The resulting state will be halfway between the ideal one and an oligarchy, retaining respect for authority and emphasizing military training and service, but giving key government positions to soldierly types, rather than the most intelligent. Lacking a philosophical education, the Guardians will love money and amass private wealth.

3   *The Timarchic Character (pp. 282–4)*

He will be self-willed, badly educated, ambitious for public office and money-loving.

4   Oligarchy (pp. 284–7)

Private wealth destroys timocracy. The greedy ruling class values money more than goodness, and introduces legislation, imposing property qualifications for public office, which establishes an oligarchy. The poor are excluded from government, even if well fitted for it, and society is split into rich and the poor. It cannot wage war, because the oligarchs fear rebellion, and people take on a variety of jobs, ending specialization. As people can sell what they own, and exist without any real function in society, a drone class of beggars and criminals appears.

5   The Oligarchic Character (pp. 287–90)

Oligarchic man values money above everything else. He has a veneer of respectability, but lacks firm moral principles, and cheats, if he can get away with it.

6   Democracy (pp. 290–4)

Oligarchy ends, because pursuit of wealth and self-discipline are incompatible. Some rulers become indebted through reckless expenditure, and start to consider revolution; a luxurious lifestyle enfeebles the rest. Democracy comes into being when the poor overthrow the rulers of this faction-ridden society, and give everybody equal rights and opportunities of office. In the short term, democracy's liberty, freedom of speech and diversity seem attractive, but it neglects careful training of future politicians. An anarchic form of society, it treats people as equal, even when they are not.

7   *The Democratic Character (pp. 294–8)*

Failings in the education system mean that young people are ignorant and lack true principles. The drone class, whose lives are ruled by indulgence of unnecessary desires and pursuit of pleasure, increases in size.

8   *Tyranny (pp. 298–308)*

Democracy is destroyed by excessive pursuit of liberty. Government falls into the hands of bad leaders from the drone class, who flatter the public. Laws are not enforced, while the rest of society divides into those who make themselves rich and the mass of the people. The political leaders tax the rich, hang on to what they can, and bribe the masses with what remains. The rich get fed up with being taxed, and oppose the government. From the confusion, a popular leader emerges, who is given the task of restoring order. Eventually, he becomes power-crazed, begins a class war against the rich, builds up a personal bodyguard, and stamps out opposition. Originally the champion of the people's liberty, he subjects them to harsh servitude.

9   *The Tyrannical Character (pp. 308–14)*

Tyrannical man unites drunkenness, lust and madness. Addicted to extravagant living, he borrows and steals whatever he wants. He is the worst type and a perfect specimen of injustice.

10   *The Types of Character and Their Degrees of Happiness* (pp. 314–30)

(a) They rank in happiness in the order they were discussed (pp. 314–19)

The tyrannical state is the most unhappy, while none is happier than the philosopher kingship. The philosopher king, sovereign over himself, and the most just man, is the happiest, while the tyrant, the most unjust and the worst, is always wretched.

(b) The life of the just man and the philosopher is pleasanter than any other (pp. 319–23)

People divide into three basic types, according to whether they are motivated by knowledge, success or gain, and each would choose his own way of life as the pleasantest. However, the philosopher is best placed to judge, as he is the one who combines intelligence and experience, and has most experience of the pleasures associated with all three ways of life. The most significant pleasures are those associated with knowledge, so the philosopher is right to prefer his own way of life. This is followed by the soldier's, with a life devoted to pursuit of gain last.

(c) The philosopher's pleasures are the most real (pp. 323–9)

What belongs to the realm of unchanging and eternal truth is more truly real than what belongs to the realm of change and mortality; and what supplies bodily needs is less true and less real than what supplies mental needs. But those who are ignorant of wisdom and goodness do not know this, so the pleasures of the masses, who are ruled by their desires, are mere phantoms of true pleasure. Any pursuit of gain and ambition must be guided by knowledge and reason. All the elements in a mind ruled by the philosophic element will be just, and each will fulfil its proper function. But, if one of the other elements predominates, false pleasures will be pursued. The greatest danger arises when the element furthest removed from philosophy and reason is in control, as occurs when tyrannical desires predominate.

(d) The tyrant is 729 times more unhappy than the philosopher king (pp. 329–30)

In the grip of spurious pleasures, the inferiority of the tyrant's way of life is hard to describe. Mathematically, the philosopher's life is seven hundred and twenty-nine times more pleasant than the tyrant's, highlighting the gulf between the just and unjust man in terms of pleasure and pain.

11   Conclusion (pp. 330–4)

Wrongdoing does not pay. The human personality is like three creatures, a many-headed beast, a lion and a man, merged into one. Saying it is advantageous to do wrong is to say that free rein should be given to the many-headed beast, and encouragement to the lion, while the man should be starved. To say that being just is advantageous is to say we should strengthen the man within us, so he controls the many-headed beast, and makes the lion an ally. Doing wrong enslaves our most divine part to the most abominable. It may bring wealth and power, but it makes a worse person. The intelligent man will aim at self-control, justice and understanding. And (Socrates adds) such a man will enter politics in the society he has described.

Part X   Theory of Art (pp. 335–53)

1   *Art and Illusion (pp. 335–45)*

Socrates argues that the work of artists and poets is at third remove from reality. They do not represent things as they actually are, but their superficial appearance. Homer may have written about military strategy and public administration, but he did not reform a state's constitution, or command an army. Poets produce a superficial likeness of the subjects they treat, including human excellence, but the magic of poetry gives the false impression that they have something worthwhile to say.

2   *The Appeal of Art and Poetry (pp. 345–9)*

Dramatic poetry appeals to some of the worst human tendencies. We feel grief at the loss of somebody close to us, but reason demands we show restraint. But the dramatic poet directs his work towards our irrational element, urging us to indulge our feelings. He finds it easier to portray emotional characters, rather than reasonable ones, thus reinforcing the lower elements of the human personality at the expense of reason.

3   *The Effects of Poetry and Drama (pp. 349–53)*

Poetry and drama can corrupt people, by encouraging indulgence of instinctive desires we normally restrain. This seems all right, because plays are about other people. We also laugh at jokes on stage, which we would be ashamed to make ourselves. Poetry's only role in the state should be to honour the gods and praise good men.

Part XI   The Immortality of the Soul and the Rewards of Goodness (pp. 354–68)

1   *The Soul Immortal (pp. 354–8)*

Socrates argues that the soul is immortal. It is made evil by injustice, indiscipline and ignorance, but its particular evils do not destroy it, as the body's particular evils, like disease, destroy it; and it cannot be harmed by bodily evils. As it is immortal, the same souls have always existed: their number cannot increase or decrease. To see what it is really like, we need to see it in the pure state that reason reveals to us, and imagine what it could become, if it pursued its love of wisdom wholeheartedly.

2   *The Rewards of Goodness in this Life (pp. 358–60)*

Justice is the best thing for our true self, and is rewarded by the gods (who know who is just or unjust) and men. The just can expect all the blessings of heaven; the unjust the opposite. In this life, the just will receive rewards and a good reputation.

3   *The Myth of Er (pp. 361–8)*

(a) The just man's rewards in the life after death (pp. 361–3)

Socrates tells the story of Er, to show what will happen to the just and unjust after death. Killed in battle, Er came back to life, and described his experiences in the other world. He witnessed souls being judged, and the just being sent up to the sky and the unjust down into the earth. He saw souls coming down from the sky, or up from the earth, and heard their discussions of the delights of heaven and underground sufferings, which lasted a thousand years.

(b) The structure of the universe (pp. 363–8)

The souls were told that they were to begin another round of mortal life, and must choose the life they would lead, taking full responsibility for their choice. Thus, it is important to discover how to lead a just and good life, and to retain this knowledge, when entering the other world, to avoid the temptations of wealth and power. Er described how some souls chose precipitately, immediately regretting their choice, while others, who had learned from their sufferings, chose carefully. After forgetting everything about their previous life and experiences in heaven or hell, they were sent on to their births.

Socrates urges the importance of always being mindful of the immortality of our souls and the need to pursue justice and wisdom. Only thus will all be well with us in this life and the next.

Glossary

Absolution. Forgiveness of sins.

Academy (the). University, founded by Plato in the 380s BC, where the educational programme of *The Republic* was followed, and which Aristotle attended.

Adeimantus. One of Plato's elder brothers, who takes a leading part in the dialogue.

Administrative occupation. Post in administration/government.

Afterlife. Life after death. Plato fears that gloomy accounts of the afterlife in Greek poems will lead to fear of death and unwillingness to fight in battle (Part III 1 (b)).

Analogy. Drawing a parallel between two things on the basis of similarities between them.

Analogy of the Divided Line. This provides a further illustration of the two orders of reality (the intelligible and the visible), discussed in the Simile of the Sun, and the states of mind that correspond to them (Part VII 6).

Anarchic form of society. Democracy is anarchic, because governments do not impose, and people do not submit to, authority (Part IX 6).

Aristocracy. Government by the best people, as in a state governed by the philosopher rulers of *The Republic*.

Aristotle (384–322 BC). Greek philosopher, student of Plato and author of such books as the *De Interpretatione*, *Nicomachean Ethics* and the *Metaphysics*.

Arithmetic. One of five mathematical subjects future philosophers need to study (Part VIII 2 (a)).

Artisan(s). Skilled worker.

Glossary

Asclepius. Greek god of medicine and son of Apollo.

Assembly. The Athenian Assembly, which all citizens (adult males) could attend and where they could vote. Plato condemns behaviour there (yelling of approval and disapproval), which may lead young men (including potential philosophers and leaders) to attach too much importance to popular opinion (Part VII 3). See also democracy below.

Assumption(s). What is taken to be true for the purposes of enquiry or argument.

Astronomy. One of five mathematical subjects future philosophers need to study and valuable for its mathematical challenges, not observation of the stars (Part VIII 2 (d)).

Athens. Greek city-state, which played a major part in defeating the Persian invasions of Greece, established a democratic system of government, and created an empire, based on sea power. See also Peloponnesian War below.

Atropos. One of the three fates.

Audible concords. Musical chords, groups of notes.

Auxiliaries. Assistant Guardians, who will help the Rulers carry out decisions, and serve in the army.

Bad pleasures. If good is defined as pleasure, there can (logically) be no such thing as a bad pleasure (Part VII 5).

Barbarian(s). Non-Greeks.

Being and non-being. Knowledge is concerned with what is the case, ignorance with what is not; the object of opinion lies between the two (Part VII 2).

Belief. State of mind that relates to the originals of things in the visible world (Part VII 6). See also Analogy of the Divided Line.

Bendis. Thracian moon goddess, identified with Artemis, whose temple was at the Piraeus.

Bond of heaven. A shaft of light, around the heaven, which keeps it together.

Businessmen. The third class in the ideal state. See also Guardians, Rulers and Auxiliaries.

Cephalus. Polemarchus' father, whose definition of justice sparks the discussion in *The Republic*.

Charmantides. Present during the dialogue, but does not take part.

Children for the state. The Guardians breed to produce the future leaders of the state, not to create a family (Part VI 2).

City. City-state, such as Athens.

Civilized society. Advanced society, with a relatively high standard of living, which requires professional administration and a trained army (Part II 2)

Class war. Conflict between the different classes in society.

Cleitophon. Present during the dialogue and makes a brief contribution.

Clotho. One of the three fates.

Composed of parts. Unlike the body, the soul is not composed of parts, but is indivisible and immortal (Part XI 1).

Consequences. Results. Glaucon argues that wisdom and health are goods that are sought both for their own sake and their consequences (Part I 4 (a)).

Constitution (political). Principles, laws by which a state is governed.

Convention. Practice or rule, based on general agreement. Adeimantus argues (Part I 4 (b)) that injustice is condemned by convention, but people behave unjustly, if they can get away with it.

Conventional opinion(s). Generally held, traditional views, as about what is right and wrong, which children are taught by their parents.

Copulate. Have sexual intercourse.

Correct belief. The user of something knows about it; its maker, relying on his knowledge, has a correct belief; poets and artists have neither (Part X 1).

Cube. Solid body with six equal square sides.

Curriculum. Course of study in school or university. Plato sets out the educational programme future Guardians will follow in Parts III and VIII of *The Republic*.

Defective offspring. Children with poor health or mental weakness.

Democracy. Government by the people and one of Plato's imperfect societies (Part IX 6). Athenian democracy was direct (not representative) and limited.

Devoted to a common interest. Free of family ties and private property, the Guardians will regard all members of their own class as brothers and sisters, and will devote their energies to service of the state (Part VI 2).

Dialectic. Process of discussion and argument that enables those following it to gain access to the intelligible world, and to see the form of the good (Part VIII 3).

Dialectician. One who practises/engages in dialectic.

Dispose of it as a creature that must not be reared. Guardians, who produce children outside their prescribed breeding ages, must dispose of them (Part VI 2).

Divine order. See forms below.

Dramatic poetry. Plato criticizes it, because it appeals to the irrational elements in the human personality, not reason.

Drone(s). The class of idlers and criminal types, produced by an oligarchic state, and which becomes powerful in a democratic one (Part IX 4–8).

Empiricism/empirical/empiricist. That which relates to, is based on, experience. Empiricists maintain that (sense) experience is the (principal) source of knowledge.

Equal civil rights. All members of a state having equal rights.

Essential nature of beauty itself. The form of beauty.

Essential nature of each thing. See forms below.

Eternal. What has always existed, and always will exist.

Eternal reality. The intelligible realm/world.

Eternal unchanging things. See forms below.

Euthydemus. Polemarchus' brother.

Evidence for judgement (of the soul). Souls are judged, and sent to heaven or the underground world, on the basis of the record of past deeds they carry (Part XI 3 (a)).

Evil. That which is opposed to good, and damages human well-being.

External influences. Outside influences/forces.

Fellow citizens. The ideal state will engender feelings of unity among its members, so rulers and ruled will genuinely regard each other as fellow citizens (Part VI 2).

Forgetful River. River Lethe.

Form of beauty. The unchanging form of beauty, in the intelligible realm, which makes particular things beautiful, and with which people need to be familiar, to make judgements about beauty (Part VII 2).

Form of the good. The form of the good has the same relation to intelligible objects in the intelligible world as the sun has to visible objects in the visible world, and it is the source of reality, truth and goodness. Only those (philosophers) who have seen it possess the highest form of knowledge; know what the good is in itself; and can say authoritatively what is good, right and just. Thus, they must govern the state (Parts VII and VIII).

Forms. Plato held that individual things in the ordinary, visible world, which we experience through our senses, acquire their identity by being (in some way) copies of the unchanging forms of these things in the intelligible realm, to which only our minds can give us access. Thus, something is round by being a copy of, or participating in, the form of roundness. However, it will not be perfectly round, but will only approximate to roundness. This is a dualistic view of reality, as it holds that there are two orders or levels of reality. Only those who, by a long process of study and discussion (dialectic), gain access to the intelligible world possess the highest form of knowledge (Part VII).

Four sections of the line. See the Analogy of the Divided Line (Part VII 6).

Four states of mind. Intelligence, reason, belief and illusion (Part VII 6).

Glaucon. One of Plato's elder brothers, who takes a leading part in the dialogue.

Gods/god. Plato refers to both 'gods' and 'god', but this does not mean that he believed in only one god, rather than the many in which the Greeks believed. He wants the gods to be portrayed positively, so that people (especially the young) will be inspired to follow their example (Part III 1 (a)).

Good things of life. Purely physical pleasures and wealth, which can distract philosophers from pursuit of truth.

Guardian class/Guardians. The ruling class of the ideal state, whose philosophical knowledge equips them to govern.

Guardian spirit. Spirit who will guide the soul through life after its rebirth.

Heroes. Outstanding mythical or historical figures, whose deeds featured in Greek poetry. Plato (Part III 1 (b)) wants them portrayed as models on which people can base their lives.

Hesiod (possibly eighth century BC). Greek poet and author of *Works and Days*.

Highest category (of goods). Those that are sought both for their own sake and their consequences.

Highest form of knowledge. See form of the good and forms above.

Homer (possibly ninth century BC). Greek epic poet, who is regarded as the author of the *Iliad* and the *Odyssey*.

Ideal state. The state, described in *The Republic*, which will be governed by philosophers.

Illusion. Seeing something that does not really exist. The state of mind corresponding to the shadows and reflections of things in the visible world (Part VII 6).

Images. The shadows and reflections of things in the visible world.

Immortal. Not dying, living on for ever.

Immutable. Unchangeable.

Immutable realities. See forms above.

Impeachment(s). Accusation of crime against the state.

Indignation. One of the three elements in the human personality, which assists reason in controlling the irrational appetite (Part V 2).

Infer. Conclude one thing from something else.

Inferior Guardians. Less intelligent Guardians with limited leadership qualities.

Innate. Inborn, in one's nature.

Instinctive desires. Natural, innate desires.

Intelligible. That which is discovered, known about, by the mind, intellect.

Intelligible realm/world. See forms and form of the good above.

Irrational appetite. The element in the human personality where desires and urges are located, and which needs to be controlled (Part V 2).

Irreversible threads of the soul's destiny. Having made its choice about its future life, the soul's destiny is irreversible.

Justice/just. Generally, treating people fairly, people being treated fairly or receiving their due. A large part of *The Republic* is devoted to discussion of the nature of justice, and justice in society/the state and the individual.

Keeping numbers constant and maintaining the size of the state. The Rulers must not allow the state to have so many citizens that it loses its sense of unity (Part VI 2).

Kind of infusion. A pouring or instilling of something into something else.

Knowledge. See forms, form of the good, being and non-being above and philosophers below.

Knowledge while the others have only opinions. One who is familiar with the intelligible world and has seen the form of the good.

Lachesis. One of the three Fates.

Lap of Necessity. A reference to the Fates. See Three Fates, daughters of Necessity below.

Laws and customs of society. Those of the kind of society Plato describes in *The Republic*, which is ruled by philosophers.

Law courts. As with the Assembly, Plato condemns public behaviour in them, and the effects of the excessive praise or blame given to winners and losers (Part VII 3).

Legislation. Laws, law-making: those of the ideal state.

Lethe. River in Hades, from which souls about to be reborn drink, in order to forget their previous existence.

Luxurious lifestyle. The Guardians must avoid a self-indulgent way of life, which will make them sickly and unfit for leadership and military service (Part III 2).

Lysias (fifth–fourth centuries BC). Polemarchus' brother, orator and writer of speeches for litigants.

Magnificent myth. The myth about the origin of the ideal state, designed to foster unity, and acceptance of their particular role, among its citizens (Part IV 1).

Many-headed beast. Plato's metaphor for the irrational appetite, which is one element in the human personality (Part IX 11).

Masses (the). Ordinary, uneducated people.

Glossary

Monarchy. Government by single ruler, such as a king or queen, which Plato (Part V 4) considers an acceptable form of government for his ideal state.

Moral conviction. Belief that one should do the right thing for its own sake, not for personal advantage or to enhance one's reputation.

Multiplicity and change. The nature of the visible world. Those who are immersed in it, and ignorant of the intelligible world, cannot attain knowledge (Part VII 2 (b)).

Natural capacity(ies). Intelligence, ability, which Plato thinks are similarly distributed in men and women (Part VI 1).

Necessary/unnecessary (of desires). Plato (Part IX 7) distinguishes between necessary desires (as for food), which are essential to support life, and unnecessary ones (as for a luxurious diet), which can be physically and psychologically harmful.

New social system. That of the ideal state, described in *The Republic*.

Niceratus. Present at the dialogue; son of Nicias, Athenian statesman and soldier.

No clear standard of right and good. Those who have not seen the form of the good, and are not fit to govern.

Object of opinion. Something that lies between what is and what is not (Part VII 2 (a)). See opinion below.

Objects of intelligence. See forms above.

Observe the prohibitions we mentioned. System of preventing members of the Guardian class from breeding with their own parents or children (Part VI 2).

Odysseus. The mythical King of Ithaca, who features in Homer's *Iliad* and whose return home from Troy is told in his *Odyssey*.

Oligarchy. Government by the few (usually leading citizens) and one of the imperfect societies (Part IX 4).

Glossary

Opinion. Opinion lies between knowledge and ignorance. Those who see beautiful objects or just acts, but not beauty or justice themselves (the forms), have opinions about, not knowledge of, them (Part VII 2 (a)).

Orbits. The orbits of the sun, moon and planets. See also whorl(s) below.

Originals of the images. Animals and plants in the visible world.

Paradoxical theory. One that appears contradictory/opposed to common sense, but in which there is truth.

Particular beautiful and good things. Individual examples of these things in the ordinary world. See forms above.

Particular evil (of each thing). Each thing has a particular evil that destroys it, as disease does the body, but this does not apply to the soul (Part XI 1).

Particular good (of each thing). Each thing has its particular good, which preserves it (Part XI 1).

Passions and pleasures of the masses. The enthusiasms and (generally physical) pleasures, preferred by ordinary people, which will be very different from those of philosophers.

Patterns of life. The types of life the souls choose before they are reborn.

Peloponnesian War. War between Athens and Sparta (and their allies) for supremacy in Greece, which began in 431 BC and ended in 404 BC with the defeat of Athens.

Pericles (c. 500–429 BC). Athenian statesman, who developed Athenian democracy and dominated Athenian politics for the 30 years before his death, which took place just after the start of the Peloponnesian War.

Phantoms of true pleasure. The illusions of pleasure that people experience when they pursue purely physical pleasures.

Philosopher. One who studies and practises/teaches philosophy. For Plato, it is one who understands the true nature of reality (Part VII). See forms and form of the good above.

Philosophers become kings in this world/philosopher king(s). The central argument of *The Republic*: that the ideal state can only be created if philosophers become kings, or those who currently rule become philosophers.

Philosophic disposition. Willingness to treat fellow-citizens with gentleness – a characteristic that the Guardians must have (Part II 3).

Philosophy. Literally, love of wisdom. The study of ultimate reality, what really exists, the most general principles of things. See also forms, form of the good and philosopher above.

Piraeus (the). Principal port of Athens, situated on a peninsula, five miles southwest of Athens and heavily fortified.

Plain of Lethe. See Lethe above.

Plane geometry. One of the five mathematical subjects that future philosophers need to study (Part VIII 2 (b)).

Pleasure. Glaucon (Part I 4 (a)) defines pleasure as a good that is desired for its own sake, not its consequences; Socrates (Part VII 5) points out that ordinary people (who are not philosophers) make the mistake of thinking that pleasure is the (only) good.

Plurality. More than one. The benefit of studying arithmetic (Part VIII 2 (a)) is that it enables students to see a thing as both a unit and an unlimited plurality.

Polemarchus. Inhabitant of Piraeus, businessman, who participates in the early stages of the dialogue, which takes place in his house.

Popular leader. A leader chosen by the people to restore order in the state, but who often becomes an oppressive tyrant (Part IX 8).

Principle. Basic truth, law or rule.

Private property. The Guardians are not allowed to have any, so that they concentrate on governing, rather than pursuing their own interests (Part IV 2).

Probity. Uprightness of character.

Professional army. One consisting of full-time, career soldiers.

Professional skill. The specialist skill(s) of a particular occupation, such as medicine.

Psychological constitution is incurably corrupt. Those too irredeemably criminal or anti-social to be good citizens of the ideal state should be killed (Part III 2).

Punishments for offences committed in a former life. After physical death, the soul is rewarded in heaven, or punished underground, and then reborn (Part XI 2).

Reactionaries. Those who are opposed to political or social change, and wish to restore society to its previous condition.

Real nature (of something)/reality/eternal reality. See forms above.

Real pedigree herd. The Rulers must enable the most intelligent and capable Guardians to breed more often than the others, to ensure the production of able and healthy children (Part VI 2).

Realm of change. The visible world.

Realm of the spiritual and divine. World of the gods.

Reason. The reflective element in the mind (Part V 2).

Refractory. Resisting discipline or control.

Remission. Forgiveness of sins.

Rulers. The eldest and most intelligent members of the Guardian class, who have seen the form of the good, and who are therefore fitted to govern the state.

Sacred. (Treated as) religious. The marriage festivals must be regarded as religious ceremonies (Part VI 2).

Sacrifice(s). Principal part of worship of Greek gods which, in tributary sacrifice, involved the worshipper giving something (an animal) to the god.

Sense-perception. Perceiving things through the senses. Unlike empiricists, Plato did not believe that sense-perception (our experience of the visible world) can be the basis of knowledge. See forms above.

Sensible world. See visible realm/world.

Serfs and menials. If the Guardians are allowed to pursue private profit, they will turn the other citizens into a semi-slave class (Part IX 2).

Simile. Comparing things, for purposes of explanation or illustration.

Simile of the Cave. This illustrates how the mind can ascend from the visible world to the intelligible world, and see the form of the good (Part VII 7).

Simile of the Sun. See Sun (the) below.

Simonides (c. 556–c. 468 BC). Greek poet, who was well known for his moral sayings.

Single forms of beauty and goodness. See form of the good and form of beauty above.

Socrates. (c. 470–399 BC). Greek philosopher, who features in the works of Plato, and who devoted his life to the pursuit of philosophical truth. He was executed by the Athenian authorities for undermining belief in the gods and corrupting youth. He did not write any philosophical works himself, and so much of what is known about him comes from Plato.

Solid geometry. One of the five mathematical subjects that future philosophers need to study (Part VIII 2 (c)).

Soul. The indestructible and immortal spiritual element within human beings, which is reborn after a period in heaven or the underground world (Part XI 1).

Sparta/Spartan. Athens' great rival in Greece, it was dominated by a hereditary military class. It has some features in common with Plato's ideal state, but was what he calls a timarchy (Part IX 1, 2). See also Peloponnesian War above.

Spindle of Necessity. Plato saw the universe as earth-centred, with sun, moon and planets revolving around it. See also whorl(s) below.

Spurious types of pleasure. Bogus pleasures.

State(s). Organized political community: here, the city-states of ancient Greece, such as Athens.

Sun (the). In the famous Simile of the Sun, Plato compares the form of the good, and its role and effects in the intelligible world, to the sun, and its role and effects in the visible world (Part VII 5 (b)).

The same souls must always have existed. As the soul is immortal and pre-existent (Part XI 1), the number of souls remains constant.

Thrasymachus of Chalcedon. A well-known teacher of rhetoric who, in *The Republic*, identifies justice with the interests of the strong and powerful.

Three classes. The three classes of the ideal state: Rulers, Auxiliaries and businessmen.

Three elements of the human personality. Reason, irrational appetite and spirit or indignation (Part V 2).

Three Fates, daughters of Necessity. Daughters of Night or possibly of Zeus (supreme god) and Themis (one of Zeus' officers).

Throne of Necessity. Where the future lives of the souls about to be reborn are determined.

Timarchy/timocracy. An imperfect society, resembling that of Sparta, which develops if the Guardians begin to pursue private profit (Part IX 2).

Tragedian(s). Writer of tragic poetry or plays. Plato severely criticizes these, and their effects on education and the development of character (Part X 1–3).

Trained soldiers. See professional army above.

True opinion. Having a true opinion without understanding is like being a blind man on the right road (Part VII 5 (a)). See opinion and object of opinion above.

Truth. See form of the good, forms, philosopher and philosophy above.

Twilight world of change and decay. The visible world, which we know through our senses.

Two orders of things, the visible and the intelligible. The visible world and the intelligible world.

Tyranny. Government by a tyrant, and one of the imperfect societies (Part IX 8).

Tyrant. An absolute, and usually oppressive, ruler.

Unit. Single number, thing.

Upper world. The world outside the cave. See the Simile of the Cave above.

Very first principle (the). The form of the good.

Visible. What can be seen: objects in the ordinary world.

Visible realm/world. See forms above.

Vision of the good. The form of the good.

Whorl(s). A disc on a spindle. The rims of the various whorls (of the spindle of necessity) represent the orbits of the sun, moon and planets around the earth, which is at the centre of the universe.

World of change. The visible world.

Wrong to sell other Greeks into slavery. Plato wanted to see unity among the Greek states, so that instead of fighting and making slaves of each other, they fought the barbarians (Part VI 3).

The Briefly Series